Predictive Eco-Cruise Control (ECC) System: Model Development, Modeling, and Potential Benefits

Prepared by

Virginia Tech Transportation Institute

The Pennsylvania State University ❖ University of Maryland
University of Virginia ❖ Virginia Polytechnic Institute and State
University ❖ West Virginia University

1. Report No. VT-2009-03 & MAUTC-2008-01	2. Government Accession No.	3. Recipient's Catalog No.
4. Title and Subtitle Predictive Eco-Cruise Control (ECC) System: Model Development, Modeling, and Potential Benefits	**5. Report Date** Feb, 19, 2013	
	6. Performing Organization Code	
7. Author(s) Hesham A. Rakha, Kyoungho Ahn, and Sangjun Park	**8. Performing Organization Report No.**	
9. Performing Organization Name and Address Virginia Tech Transportation Institute (VTTI) 3500 Transportation Research Plaza, Blacksburg, VA 24061 Phone number:(540) 231-1500	**10. Work Unit No. (TRAIS)**	
	11. Contract or Grant No. DTRT07-G-0003	
12. Sponsoring Agency Name and Address US Department of Transportation Research & Innovative Technology Admin UTC Program, RDT-30 1200 New Jersey Ave., SE Washington, DC 20590	**13. Type of Report and Period Covered** Final, 12/1/2008 – 12/31/2012	
	14. Sponsoring Agency Code	

15. Supplementary Notes

16. Abstract

The research develops a reference model of a predictive eco-cruise control (ECC) system that intelligently modulates vehicle speed within a pre-set speed range to minimize vehicle fuel consumption levels using roadway topographic information. The study includes five basic tasks: (a) develop a vehicle powertrain model that can be easily implemented within eco-driving tools; (b) develop a simple fuel consumption model that computes instantaneous vehicle fuel consumption levels based on power exerted; (c) evaluate manual driving and conventional cruise control (CC) driving using field-collected data; (d) develop a predictive ECC system that uses the developed vehicle powertrain and fuel consumption models; and (e) evaluate the potential benefits of the proposed predictive ECC system on a pre-trip and fleet-aggregate basis. This study develops a predictive ECC system that can save fuel and reduce CO2 emissions using road topography information. The performance of the system is tested by simulating a vehicle trip on a section of Interstate 81 in the state of Virginia. The results demonstrate fuel savings of up to 15 percent with execution times within real time. The study found that the implementation of the predictive ECC system could help achieving better fuel economy and air quality.

17. Key Words Fuel consumption, Emission, Eco Driving, Eco Cruise Control, Fuel consumption modeling, Powertrain modeling	18. Distribution Statement No restrictions. This document is available from the National Technical Information Service, Springfield, VA 22161	

19. Security Classif. (of this report) Unclassified	20. Security Classif. (of this page) Unclassified	21. No. of Pages 91 pages	22. Price

Table of Contents

EXECUTIVE SUMMARY

The research presented in this report develops a reference model of a predictive eco-cruise control (ECC) system that intelligently modulates vehicle speed within a pre-set speed range to minimize vehicle fuel consumption levels using roadway topographic information. The study includes five basic tasks: (a) develop a vehicle powertrain model that can be easily implemented within eco-driving tools; (b) develop a simple fuel consumption model that computes instantaneous vehicle fuel consumption levels based on power exerted; (c) evaluate manual driving and conventional cruise control (CC) driving using field-collected data; (d) develop a predictive ECC system that uses the developed vehicle powertrain and fuel consumption models; and (e) evaluate the potential benefits of the proposed predictive ECC system on a pre-trip and fleet-aggregate basis.

A vehicle powertrain model is closely related to eco-driving research since a vehicle's ability to accelerate with reasonable accuracy and excellent computational efficiency is an important factor in eco-driving techniques. There have been a significant number of studies on the modeling of vehicle engines and controls. Specifically, these models were developed with a focus on engine design, analysis, and control. While these models are sufficient for their intended purposes, they are not adequate for use in microscopic traffic simulation software for two reasons. Ni and Henclewood [3] indicate that typical engine models are computationally intensive and cannot be integrated within car-following, lane-changing, and gap acceptance algorithms which are critical for traffic simulation models. Second, these models require proprietary parameters that are difficult to obtain and, in some instances, require gathering field data for the entire envelope of operation of a vehicle. Thus, the development of a vehicle powertrain model that can be utilized for traffic simulation models is a new challenge for traffic engineers.

The research presented in this study develops a simple vehicle powertrain model that can be easily implemented in other applications such as fuel consumption models and microscopic traffic simulation software. A key input to the powertrain model used in this study is the driver throttle input. This study focuses on the modeling of a vehicle powertrain system assuming that the driver input is known.

The proposed powertrain model starts with the driver throttle and brake input. Using the driver's throttle input, the engine speed is computed utilizing a simple regression model that was developed in this study using field observations of engine speed and throttle level. In the case of a manual transmission system the gear selection is made directly using the engine speed. Alternatively, in the case of an automatic transmission system the torque converter is modeled prior to the transmission system. The engine speed and torque are then used to compute the vehicle power using a parabolic vehicle engine model that was developed by Ni and Henclewood [3]. The vehicle acceleration is then computed considering a point mass vehicle dynamics model. The vehicle speed and position are estimated by solving the second order differential equation. This simple model can be calibrated using engine and powertrain parameters that are publicly available without the need for field data collection. The model was demonstrated to produce vehicle acceleration, speed, and position that are consistent with field observations. The developed powertrain model estimated the vehicle power within reasonable accuracy. The model estimates instantaneous vehicle power within 1.7 to 20.2 percent error range when compared to the field measured power data for test vehicles.

A new power-based microscopic fuel consumption model is also developed in this study. While various eco-driving tools have been developed recently, most models use traditional fuel consumption models to estimate the benefit of their eco-driving system. However, traditional fuel consumption models typically use the average speed as an input variable, which may not be enough to quantify sharp accelerations and aggressive driving behaviors. Consequently, this study develops a fuel consumption model that can estimate instantaneous fuel consumption in order to improve the accuracy of fuel estimation.

There are a number of tools available that can estimate vehicle emissions and fuel consumption levels. Most of these models use vehicle tractive power and/or velocity as explanatory variables. These models appear to be simple and easy to implement; however, the calibration of the model parameters is not a simple task and typically requires vehicle-specific data that are not publicly available. Some of the factors are almost impossible to obtain. Compromising between simplicity and accuracy has always been a difficult task for any model. Consequently, the research focuses on developing a simple fuel consumption model that can be calibrated using publicly available data and also can be implemented within energy-saving driving assistance tools or microscopic traffic simulation software.

This study presents a new power-based microscopic fuel consumption model entitled the Virginia Tech Comprehensive Power-based Fuel Consumption Model (VT-CPFM). The developed fuel consumption model overcomes two major drawbacks of existing fuel consumption and emission models, namely: (a) they produce a bang-bang control through the use of a linear power model (i.e., the optimum fuel consumption requires a full throttle acceleration); and (b) the calibration of model parameters cannot be done using publicly available data, thus necessitating in-laboratory or field data collection. The research presented in this paper develops two simple fuel consumption models. Specifically, the models produce a continuously variable (non-bang-bang) control and are calibrated using the U.S. Environmental Protection Agency (EPA) city and highway fuel economy ratings in addition to publicly available vehicle and roadway pavement parameters.

The models estimate vehicle fuel consumption rates consistent with in-field measurements (coefficient of determination above 0.90). The study validates the VT-CPFMs by comparing the field-measured fuel consumption rates with the model estimates. Six light-duty vehicles, including four sedans and two sport utility vehicles (SUVs), were tested on a section of Interstate 81. From the comparison results, the VT-CPFMs calibrated using the city and highway fuel economy values provide reliable fuel consumption estimates. The study found that the peaks and valleys on the test run profiles in the fuel consumption estimates are consistent with the field data, demonstrating that both estimates and measurements have the same pattern depending on the engine load conditions. In addition, the models estimate CO_2 emissions that are highly correlated with field measurements (correlation coefficient greater than 0.98). The development of the VT-CPFMs attempts to bridge the existing gap between traditional power-based fuel consumption models and vehicle operational control systems such as fuel-optimized CC systems, real-time eco-driving systems, and adaptive CC systems. The proposed model can be integrated within a traffic simulation framework to quantify the energy and environmental impacts of traffic operational projects.

This study performed a field experiment to compare conventional CC driving and manual driving with regard to fuel economy. The field experiment was conducted using five vehicles on a section of Interstate 81, which comprises ±4% uphill and downhill sections. Using an Onboard Diagnostic II reader, instantaneous fuel consumption rates and other driving parameters were collected during the field tests with or without the CC enabled. The collected data were compared with regard to fuel economy, throttle control, and travel time. The study found that the CC driving improves fuel efficiency as compared to the manual driving, although there were some variations in the differences depending on the driver, the vehicle, and the direction of travel (northbound versus southbound). The average fuel economy enhancement across all the field tests was 3.3%. It is interesting to note that using CC on downhill sections resulted in better fuel economy than using it on uphill sections. The study also found that manual driving and CC driving were not significantly different from each other with regard to travel time. Statistical tests were conducted to ascertain if the differences in fuel consumption between CC driving and manual driving were statistically significant. A multiple linear regression model was fitted to the field-measured fuel consumption data to reveal the relationship of the fuel economy to other contributing factors.

This study investigates a possible fuel-saving and greenhouse emission reduction strategy using a predictive ECC system. The newly developed powertrain model and fuel consumption model are implemented into the predictive ECC system. Roadway grades have a significant impact on vehicle fuel consumption and CO_2 emission rates. On upgrade sections, vehicles exert additional power to overcome the grade resistance force, thus consuming more fuel compared to driving on a flat surface. Studies have shown that roadway grade results in significant increases in vehicle fuel consumption and emission levels [4, 5]. Park and Rakha (2006) demonstrated that a 6-percent increase in the roadway grade could increase vehicle fuel consumption levels in the range of 40 to 94 percent, and a 1-percent grade could cause 13- to 18-percent increases in fuel consumption levels [5]. A recent study claimed that the overall fuel economy of the flat route is superior to that of the hilly route by approximately 15 to 20 percent [6]. Thus, energy-efficient operations on hilly roads could produce significant savings in fuel consumption usage.

A conventional CC system allows the driver to maintain a desired speed by adjusting the vehicle throttle level. However, these traditional CC systems can result in excessive fuel usage by attempting to maintain a desired speed on upgrade and downgrade roadway segments. It is known that a small portion of trips that involve high engine load operations are responsible for a disproportionate contribution of trip emissions and fuel consumption levels [7]. Thus, if a vehicle attempts to maintain a pre-set speed on a steep uphill section, this segment could consume significant amounts of fuel and produce significant greenhouse gas (GHG) emissions.

This study develops a predictive ECC system that can save fuel and reduce CO_2 emissions using road topography information. The predictive ECC system consists of three components: a fuel consumption module, a powertrain module, and an optimization algorithm. The developed system generates an optimal throttle and speed control plan using roadway grade information obtained from a high-resolution digital map to control the vehicle speed within a pre-set speed window in a fuel-saving manner. The study found that the heuristic search algorithm finds the optimum plan more quickly with a gap in the objective function of less than 1 percent when compared to the shortest path algorithm. The performance of the system is tested by simulating a vehicle trip on a section of Interstate 81 in the state of Virginia. The results demonstrate fuel savings of up to 15 percent with execution times within real time. The simulation made assumptions for an easier interpretation of the system performance, which include: no errors in the vehicle control and topographical information feeding, and no interference by other vehicles.

Finally, the study quantifies the potential benefits of the predictive ECC system considering the variations in roadway grades, as compared to the conventional CC system. Based on the simulation results, the study found that the benefits of the predictive ECC system are maximized when vehicles travel on hillier terrains rather than mild terrains. Also, the predictive ECC system saves more fuel when the test vehicles are operated at higher target speeds as opposed to lower target speeds. Specifically, the test vehicles showed the best performance with regard to fuel consumption saving at the target speed of 120 km/h.

The study also examines the impacts of using the predictive ECC system over a New York City to Los Angeles route and found that the system can save fuel consumption in a range of 4.7 to 6.7 percent, without increasing the total travel time, when a vehicle utilizes the predictive ECC. The simulation results demonstrate that the introduction of various speed range schemes during the predictive ECC trips can significantly improve the performance of the system, enhancing vehicle fuel efficiency without increasing the total travel time.

The study quantified the potential benefits of the predictive ECC over a conventional CC system considering different roadway grade scenarios. The simulation study found if a predictive ECC system is applied to all vehicles in the United States, the average potential fuel savings were projected to be 1.04 billion gallons per year, which is equivalent to $3.12 billion per year when assuming that the price of gasoline is $3.00 per gallon. In addition, the ECC system can result in 9.2 million fewer metric tons of CO2 released into the atmosphere, assuming that 1 liter of fuel produces 2.33 kg of CO2.

The study demonstrates that the predictive ECC system can significantly improve vehicle fuel economy along various terrain sections. Since the road grade effect certainly plays a significant role in fuel consumption and CO_2 emissions, it is expected that the implementation of the predictive ECC system can help achieve better fuel economy and improve air quality.

1. SIMPLE VEHICLE POWERTRAIN MODEL FOR MODELING INTELLIGENT VEHICLE APPLICATIONS

This section develops a vehicle powertrain model that is utilized for traffic simulation software and integrated with vehicle fuel consumption and emission models. There have been several studies on the modeling of vehicle engines and controls [8-15]. Specifically, these models were developed with a focus on engine design, analysis, and control. While these models are sufficient for their intended purposes, they are not adequate for use in microscopic traffic simulation software for two reasons. Ni and Henclewood [3] indicate that typical engine models are computationally intensive and cannot be integrated within car-following, lane-changing, and gap acceptance algorithms which are critical for traffic simulation models. Second, these models require proprietary parameters that are difficult to obtain and, in some instances, require gathering field data for the entire envelope of operation of a vehicle. Thus, the development of a vehicle powertrain model that can be utilized for traffic simulation models is a new challenge for traffic engineers.

Driving an automobile is complex, given that drivers must perform lateral-directional loop closure, longitudinal loop closure, information gathering, and hazard detection. In the case of lateral directional loop closure, drivers use the steering wheel to control lane position and heading. Alternatively, in the case of longitudinal loop closure, drivers use the accelerator and brake pedal, as well as the gear shift lever and clutch in manual transmission vehicles, to control the vehicle's longitudinal position and speed. At the same time, drivers must attend to additional in-vehicle tasks associated with the instrument panel and related comfort/convenience items.

Microscopic traffic simulation software uses car-following models to capture the longitudinal motion of a vehicle and its interaction with the preceding vehicle traveling in the same lane [16, 17]. The first equation characterizes the motion of the Following Vehicle (FV) with respect to the behavior of the Lead Vehicle (LV). The second set of equations constrains the car-following behavior by ensuring that vehicle accelerations are realistic. The model can be presented by either characterizing a relationship between a vehicle's desired speed and the vehicle spacing (speed formulation), or alternatively by describing a relationship between the vehicle's acceleration and speed differential between the FV and LV (acceleration formulation). The latter formulation is typical of the well-known GM car-following models with a control variable (acceleration), a stimulus variable (speed differential), and a driver sensitivity parameter. Rakha et al. [16] demonstrate that the speed formulation is a more appropriate formulation.

In order to ensure feasible vehicle accelerations one may consider a vehicle kinematics model, a constant power vehicle dynamics model [1], a variable power vehicle dynamics model [2], or a more sophisticated gear-shifting model. A vehicle dynamics or gear-shifting modeling approach is better because the model parameters can be adjusted to reflect different weather, tire, and roadway surface conditions without the need to gather any field data.

The research presented in this paper enhances vehicle longitudinal motion modeling by developing a simple vehicle powertrain model that can be easily implemented within traffic simulation software and can be integrated with power-based vehicle fuel consumption and emission models. A key input to the powertrain model is the driver throttle input. A driver's aggressiveness is one of the important elements to represent real-world driving conditions in traffic simulation models. Thus, this study utilized the driver throttle level as a key input variable to characterize the driving behaviors on roadways. Intra- and inter-driver variability is likely present depending on the surrounding traffic conditions and the driver's psychological state (e.g., fatigued, in a hurry, or distracted). This paper, however, focuses on the modeling of a vehicle powertrain system assuming that the driver input is known. Research is currently underway to characterize driver throttle input depending on the vehicle, roadway, and surrounding traffic conditions.

1.1 Model Description

The model starts with the driver throttle and brake input, as illustrated in Figure 1. Using the driver's throttle input the engine speed is computed employing a simple regression model that was developed in this study via field observations of engine speed and throttle level. In the case of a manual transmission system, the gear selection is made directly by using the engine speed. Alternatively, in the case of an automatic transmission system, the torque converter is modeled prior to the transmission system [18]. The engine speed and torque are then used to compute the vehicle power using a parabolic vehicle engine model that was developed by Ni and Henclewood [3]. The vehicle acceleration is then computed considering a point mass vehicle dynamics model. The vehicle speed and position are estimated by solving the second order differential equation. The specifics of each of the components of the model are described in the following sections.

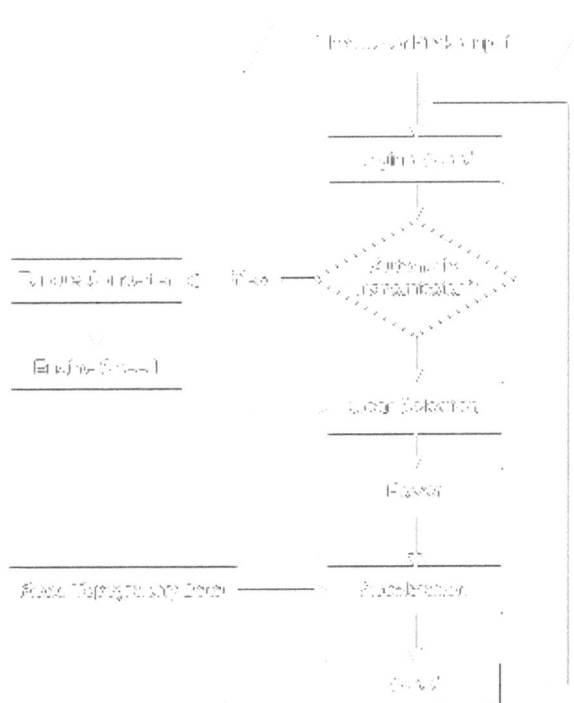

Figure 1: Proposed Model Structure

Throttle/Engine Speed Modeling

As was mentioned earlier, the task of driving an automobile is demanding given that drivers must perform lateral-directional loop closure, longitudinal loop closure, information gathering, and hazard detection. In the case of longitudinal loop closure, drivers use the accelerator and brake pedal, as well as the gear shift lever and clutch in manual transmission vehicles, to control the longitudinal position and speed of the vehicle. At the same time, drivers must attend to additional in-vehicle tasks associated with the instrument panel and related comfort/convenience items. The driver accelerator pedal input in turn affects the throttle level of the vehicle engine. The modeling of driver input entails modeling the driver accelerator pedal level and its effect on the throttle level. This two-level process can be modeled using a single model without the need to capture the accelerator pedal position. The advantage of the latter approach is that data can be gathered using On-board Diagnostic (OBD) readers without the need for cameras to capture the accelerator pedal position. This approach is used in this study.

The driver-selected throttle level results in a change in the engine speed. In an attempt to establish a relationship between the throttle level ($f(t)$) and engine speed ($w_e(t)$) at any instant (t), field data were gathered using a 1999 Ford Crown Victoria. The vehicle was powered by a 4.6 L, V-8 engine using an 87 octane fuel, rated at 200 hp @ 4250 rpm, with an electronic 4-speed automatic overdrive transmission. The vehicle, which was owned by the Virginia Tech Transportation Institute (VTTI), had a mileage of 9,500 miles at the start of the tests. An OBD reader was used to gather the driver input and engine speed. The data were gathered for typical driving along the Route 460 Bypass and Main Street in Blacksburg, VA. The 460 Bypass is a 7 km, limited access, divided highway between Christiansburg and Blacksburg, VA, while Main Street is a signalized arterial. A total of 13 trip repetitions were made in order to ensure that sufficient data were available. The data were then sorted and binned based on the throttle level. The average engine speed within each throttle level bin was then computed, and a relationship between the throttle level and engine speed was derived, as illustrated in Figure 2.

A Least Squared Error (LSE) regression was applied to the data considering the throttle level as the response variable and the engine speed as the explanatory variable. The developed model, which had a high coefficient of determination ($R^2 = 0.92$), is of the form

$$w_e(t) = (w_t + w_{idle}) \times \frac{\ln(f(t))}{\ln(f_{\min})} - w_t \qquad (1)$$

Where $w_e(t)$ is the engine speed (rpm) at any instant t; w_t is the engine speed at maximum torque (rpm); w_{idle} is the idling engine speed (rpm); $f(t)$ is the throttle position at any instant t (0~100 percent); and f_{min} is the minimum throttle position (0~100 percent). The model requires the calibration of three vehicle-specific parameters, namely: the engine speed at idling, the engine speed at maximum torque, and the minimum throttle level. The first two parameters can be easily obtained from auto manufacturer websites, while the latter parameter can either be obtained by gathering engine data using an OBD reader or assumed to be approximately 10 to 15 percent. The data demonstrated that the throttle level ranged between 15 and 65 percent for typical driving conditions.

It should be noted that additional engine data are required in order to characterize the functional relationship between the throttle level and engine speed for different vehicle types, engine sizes, engine technologies, and vehicle age/mileage. It is recommended that further research be conducted to gather these field data.

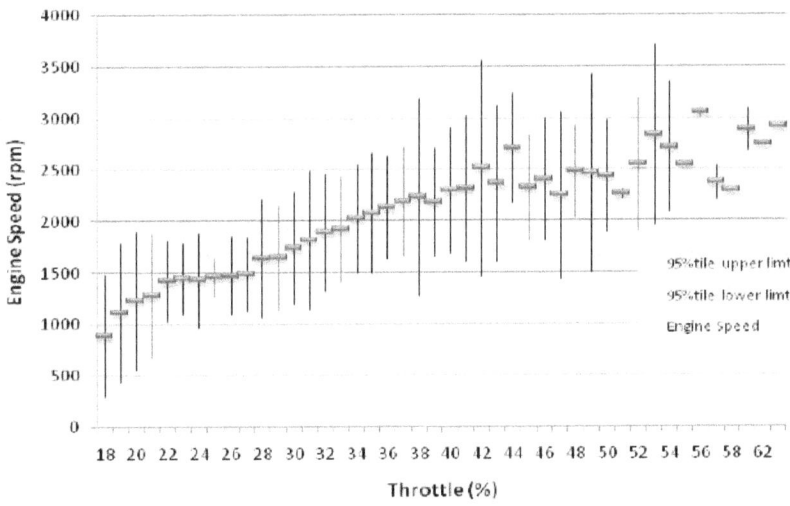

(a) Field Mean and 95% Confidence Limits

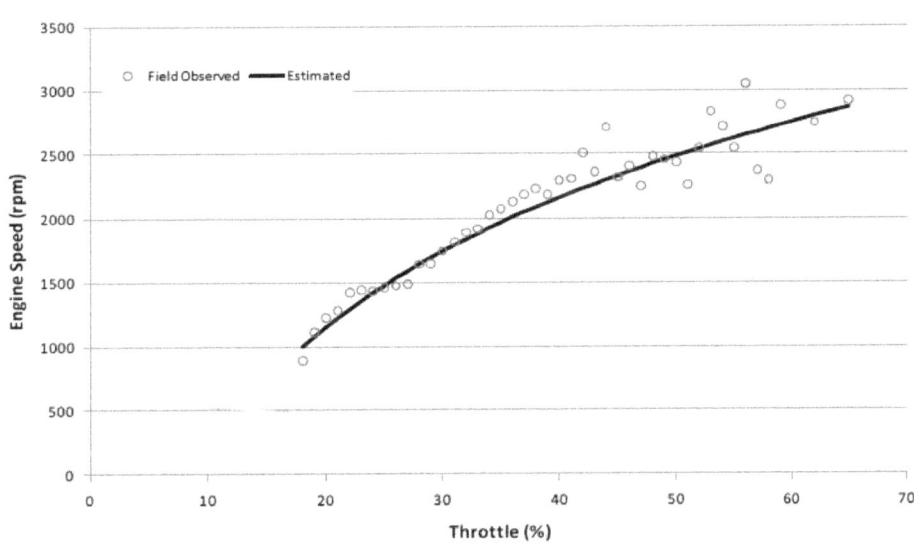

(b) Model Predictions vs. Field Observations

Figure 2: Example Throttle vs. Engine Speed Relationship

Engine Modeling

Ni and Henclewood [3] indicate that although there has been a wealth of literature published about the modeling of internal combustion (IC) engines, these models were developed with a focus on engine design, analysis, and control. While these models are sufficient for their intended purposes, they are not adequate for use in traffic simulation software for two reasons. First, they are computationally intensive and cannot be integrated within car-following, lane-changing, and gap acceptance algorithms. Second, these models require proprietary parameters that are difficult to obtain and, in some instances, require gathering field data for the entire envelope of operation of a vehicle. Ni and Henclewood [3] summarize the desired attributes of such a model as:

- Accuracy: The engine model must provide reasonable accuracy to predict engine performance with throttle and engine speed as inputs and engine power and torque as outputs. In this study accuracy is defined as providing ideal approximation for the engine behavior with quality repeatability for different engines.
- Computational efficiency: The engine model must be simple enough to facilitate on-board computing with high frequency in real time.
- Accessibility: To assist wide deployment across different vehicle platforms, the engine model should not rely on proprietary parameters and variables that are difficult to measure. All the information needed to run the model should be publicly available.
- Formulation: The engine model should be analytical. Engine models based on look-up tables are not only prohibitive to prepare for each individual vehicle but also resource-demanding in computation.
- Calibration: The engine model should be simple in order to ensure that the model calibration is easy.

Ni and Henclewood [3] presented three simple engine models. The first of these models is a polynomial model that was developed by Genta [19]. This model uses a polynomial to empirically approximate the relationship between engine power, P_e (KW), and engine speed, ω_e (rpm), as

$$P_e = \sum_{i=1}^{3} C_i \omega_e^i \tag{2}$$

where C_i, $i = 0, 1, 2, 3$ are coefficients and can be estimated from empirical engine curves. These coefficients can be estimated as

$$C_1 = 1000(60) \cdot \frac{P_{\max}}{\omega_p}, \quad C_2 = 1000(60)^2 \cdot \frac{P_{\max}}{\omega_p^2}, \quad C_3 = -1000(60)^3 \cdot \frac{P_{\max}}{\omega_p^3} \tag{3}$$

where P_{max} (KW) is the peak power and ω_p (rpm) is the engine speed at peak power.

The second model that was developed by Ni and Henclewood assumes a parabolic relationship between the engine torque, T_e (N-m), and engine speed, ω_e (rpm). Using this assumption, the relationship between engine power and speed can be written as

$$P_e = \frac{P_{\max}}{2\omega_p^2}\left(3\omega_p - \omega_t\right)w_e - \frac{P_{\max}}{2\omega_p^2(\omega_p - \omega_t)}\left(\omega_e - \omega_t\right)^2 \omega_e \tag{4}$$

where ω_t is the engine speed at peak torque (rpm). The engine torque, T_e (N-m), can be computed as

$$T_e = 60000\frac{P_e}{2\pi\omega_e} \tag{5}$$

The final model developed by Ni and Henclewood [3] is based on Bernoulli's principle. Because this model is more complicated than the other two models the model equation is not presented here. The interested reader can refer to Ni and Henclewood's paper for more detailed information [3].

Ni and Henclewood validated the three models using empirical curves for four automotive engines: a 2008 Mercedes CLS, a 2006 Honda Civic, a 2006 Pagani Zonda, and a 1964 Chevrolet Corvair. The study concluded that, in terms of computational efficiency, the three models are all acceptable with the polynomial and parabolic models being particularly efficient. In terms of accessibility, the polynomial and parabolic models were found to be excellent because they do not require any proprietary parameters or difficult-to-measure variables. All three models were equally good in terms of analytical formulation. Given that the Bernoulli model requires much effort to calibrate, while the other two models involve minimal calibration effort, the authors did not recommend the use of the Bernoulli model. The authors concluded that the parabolic model appeared to be the best among the three models when all evaluation criteria were considered. Consequently, the proposed framework uses the parabolic model that is presented in Equation (4).

Torque Converter Modeling

As was mentioned earlier, automatic transmission passenger car vehicles in North America are typically equipped with a torque converter. Wong [18] indicates that a "torque converter consists of at least three rotary elements known as the pump (impeller), the turbine, and the reactor." Wong also mentions that "the pump is connected to the engine shaft, and the turbine is connected to the output shaft of the converter, which in turn is coupled with the input shaft of the multispeed gearbox. The reactor is coupled to an external casing to provide a reaction on the fluid circulating in the converter. The function of the reactor is to enable the turbine to develop an output torque higher than the input torque of the converter, thus to obtain a torque multiplication. The reactor is usually mounted on a free wheel (one-way clutch) so that when the starting period has been completed and the turbine speed is approaching that of the pump, the reactor is in free rotation. At this point, the converter operates as a fluid coupling, with a ratio of output torque to input torque equal to 1.0." Wong summarizes the advantages of a torque converter as follows:

1. When properly matched, it will not stall the engine.
2. It provides a flexible coupling between the engine and the driven wheels (or sprockets).
3. Together with a suitably selected multispeed gearbox, it provides torque-speed characteristics that approach the ideal.

The performance characteristics of a torque converter are usually described in terms of four parameters: (a) the speed ratio, C_{sr}, which is the ratio of the output to input speed; (b) the torque ratio, C_{tr}, which is the ratio of the output to input torque; (c) the efficiency, η_c, where $\eta_c = C_{sr}C_{tr}$; and (d) the capacity factor, K_{tc} = speed/(torque)$^{0.5}$.

The torque converter was modeled as follows:

1. The capacity factor is computed as $K_{tc} = K_e = \omega_e / \sqrt{T_e}$, where ω_e is the engine (input) speed and T_e is the engine (input) torque. The engine speed is computed using Equation (1) and the engine torque is computed using Equations (4) and (5).
2. The speed ratio (C_{sr}) is computed from the relationship between K_{tc} and C_{sr}. This relationship is derived from curves in the literature [18].
3. The torque converter speed and torque ratios are computed using the relationship between C_{sr} and C_{tr} and C_{sr} and η_c, respectively. Again, these relationships were derived from the literature [18].
4. The torque converter output speed (ω_{tc}) and torque (T_{tc}) are computed as $\omega_{tc} = C_{sr}\omega_e$ and $T_{tc} = C_{tr}T_e$.
5. The power leaving the torque converter (P_{tc}) is computed as $P_{tc} = \dfrac{2\pi T_{tc}\omega_{tc}}{60000}$.

Gear Selection Modeling

Once the powertrain speed is computed the next step is to evaluate the need to shift gears through the modeling of a transmission system. Wong [18] indicates that "the term 'transmission' includes all of those systems or subsystems employed for transmitting the engine power to the driven wheels or sprockets. There are two common types of transmission for road vehicles: the manual gear transmission, and the automatic transmission with a torque converter. Other types of transmissions, such as continuous variable transmission (CVT) and hydrostatic transmission, are also in use."

Wong [18] indicates that the principal requirements for the transmission are: (a) to achieve the desired maximum speed with an appropriate engine; (b) to be able to start, fully loaded, in both forward and reverse directions on a steep gradient, typically 33 percent; and (c) to properly match the characteristics of the engine to achieve the desired operating fuel economy and acceleration characteristics.

A manual gear transmission usually consists of a clutch, a gearbox, a propeller shaft, and a drive axle with a differential (to allow relative rotation of the driven tires during turning maneuvers). The gearbox provides a number of gear reduction ratios ranging from 3 to 6 for passenger cars and 5 to 16 or more for commercial vehicles. The number of gear ratios is selected to provide the vehicle with the propulsive effort-speed characteristics as close to the ideal as possible in a cost-effective manner. The gear ratio for the highest gear is computed as

$$\xi_n = \frac{n_{el} r (1 - i)}{v_{max} \xi_{ax}}$$ (6)

where ξ_n is the gear ratio of the highest gear in the gearbox for an n-speed vehicle; n_{el} is the engine speed corresponding to the maximum speed (about 10 percent higher than the speed at maximum power); r is the rolling radius of the tire; i is the tire slip (2 to 5 percent); vmax is the maximum desired speed; and ξ_{ax} is the gear ratio in the drive axle.

The lowest gear ratio is computed so that a vehicle can accelerate on a grade at a desired acceleration rate. The formula for computing this gear ratio varies depending on whether the vehicle is front- versus rear-wheel drive. Once the highest and lowest gear ratios are determined, the remaining gear ratios are selected to establish the following relationship

$$\frac{\xi_2}{\xi_1} = \frac{\xi_3}{\xi_2} = \ldots = \frac{\xi_n}{\xi_{n-1}} = K_g$$ (7)

where $K_g = \sqrt[n-1]{\xi_n / \xi_1}$.

Gear shifting is typically controlled by shift maps that provide electronic shift points. The gear control is typically governed by various factors that include: (a) the engine speed, (b) the throttle position, (c) the pedal position, and (d) the vehicle speed. The proposed model only considers the engine speed in shifting gears. The model assumes that drivers/transmission system makes gear shifts when the vehicle reaches the engine speed at peak torque, ω_t. Downshifts are made when the vehicle reaches an engine speed of 1,500 rpm based on typical values provided in the literature (1,000 to 2,000 rpm).

Vehicle Acceleration Modeling

Once the power generated by the powertrain is computed, the vehicle acceleration at any instant *t*, *a(t)* can be estimated as

$$a(t) = \left| \frac{F(t) - R(t)}{m\left(1.04 + 0.0025\varepsilon_0(t)^2\right)} \right|$$ (8)

where $F(t)$ is the vehicle propulsive force at instant t (N); $R(t)$ is the sum of resistance forces at instant t acting on the vehicle (N); m is the vehicle mass (kg); and $\xi_0(t)$ is the final gear ratio at instant t. The powertrain propulsive force is computed as the minimum of the engine or torque converter propulsive force and the maximum frictional force that can be sustained between the vehicle's wheels on the propulsive axle and the roadway surface as

$$F(t) = \min\left[3600 \cdot \eta_d \cdot \frac{P}{v(t)}, 9.8066 \cdot m_{ta} \cdot \mu\right] \tag{9}$$

where η_d is the driveline efficiency; P is the propulsive power (equal to P_e if manual transmission or P_{tc} if automatic transmission); v is the vehicle speed one time step earlier (km/h); m_{ta} is the mass on the propulsive axle (kg); and μ is the coefficient of roadway adhesion.

The resultant resistance force acting on the vehicle at any instant t is computed as the sum of the aerodynamic, the rolling, and the grade resistance forces. The first resistance force is the aerodynamic resistance that varies as a function of the square of the air speed. Although a precise description of the various forces would involve the use of vectors, for most transportation applications scalar equations suffice if the forces are considered to only apply in the roadway longitudinal direction. The second resistance force is the rolling resistance, which is a linear function of the vehicle speed and mass. The final resistance force is the grade resistance force, which is a function of the vehicle mass and roadway grade at instant t, $G(t)$. Using the three resistance forces, the resultant resistance force can be computed as

$$R(t) = \frac{\rho}{25.92} C_D C_h A_f v^2(t) + 9.8066 m C_r \left[c_5 v(t) + c_6\right] + 9.8066 m G(t) \tag{10}$$

where ρ is the density of air at sea level and a temperature of 15°C (59°F) (equal to 1.2256 kg/m^3); C_D is the drag coefficient (unitless); C_h is a correction factor for altitude (unitless); A is the vehicle frontal area (m^2); and C_r, c_5 and c_6 are rolling resistance parameters that vary as a function of the road surface type, condition, and vehicle tires [20]. Generally, radial tires provide a resistance that is 25 percent less than that for bias ply tires.

Given that the air density varies as a function of altitude, H (m), the C_h factor can be computed as

$$C_h = 1 - 8.5 \times 10^{-5} H \tag{11}$$

Typical values of vehicle frontal areas for different vehicle types and typical drag coefficients are provided in the literature [20]. Similarly, typical values for the coefficient of roadway adhesion and the rolling resistance coefficients are provided in the literature [2, 20].

Once the acceleration is computed, the vehicle speed and position can then be computed by solving the second-order Ordinary Differential Equation (ODE) of Equation (8) numerically using a first-order Euler approximation as

$$v(t + \Delta t) = v(t) + a(t)\Delta t \text{ and } x(t + \Delta t) = x(t) + v(t)\Delta t \tag{12}$$

Finally, the engine speed can be computed as

$$\omega(t + \Delta t) = \min\left[\max\left[\frac{1000 v(t + \Delta t)\xi_0}{120\pi r (1 - i)}, \omega_{idle}\right], \omega_{red}\right] \tag{13}$$

where ω_{red} is the redline or maximum engine speed. This parameter can be easily obtained from automotive websites.

1.2 Model Validation

The validation of the proposed powertrain model was conducted using data gathered earlier along the Virginia Smart Road test facility at VTTI [1, 2]. In addition to documenting all available information about the vehicle and roadway characteristics, the data were gathered under conditions in which vehicle accelerations were not constrained by surrounding traffic. Furthermore, the drivers accelerated at the maximum possible acceleration level; thus the *f(t)* parameter was calibrating while assuming it to be constant. This section summarizes the key parameters associated with the test facility, the test vehicles, and the data collection procedures.

Test Facility

Testing of vehicles was performed on a 1.6-km (1-mile) section of the Smart Road test facility at VTTI in Blacksburg, VA. The selected test section featured a relatively straight horizontal layout with a minor horizontal curvature that had no effect on vehicle speeds, a good asphalt roadway surface, and a substantial upgrade that ranged from 6 percent at one end to 2.8 percent at the other end. Since no flat sections of significant length were available, vehicle accelerations were measured by driving vehicles uphill.

An equation characterizing the grade of the test section was derived from the elevations of 15 stations along the test section. The vertical profile of the test section was then generated by interpolating between station elevations using a cubic spline interpolation procedure at 1-m (3.28-ft) increments. The cubic spline interpolation ensured that the elevations, slopes, and slope rate of change were identical at the boundary conditions (in this case, every meter). The grade was then computed for each 1-m (3.28-ft) section. A polynomial regression model was fit to the grade data (R^2 of 0.951) to ensure a smooth transition in the roadway grade while maintaining the same vertical profile, as demonstrated in Equation (8). The regression equation also facilitated the solution of the ODE by ensuring that the grade function was continuous.

$$G(x) = 0.059628 + 3.32 \times 10^{-6}\, x - 3.79 \times 10^{-8}\, x^2 + 1.42 \times 10^{-11}\, x^3 \qquad (14)$$

Here *x* is the distance from the beginning of the test section (m) and *G(x)* is the roadway grade (m/100 m) at any location *x*.

Test Vehicles

Thirteen light-duty test vehicles were used in the study. These vehicles were selected to cover a wide range of light-duty vehicle combinations, as summarized in Table 1. As indicated in the table, the selected vehicles represent a range of sizes and a variety of U.S. Environmental Protection Agency (EPA) vehicle classes.

Table 1 presents the main characteristics of each of the light-duty vehicles and related parameters for use in the powertrain model described earlier. Below is a description of each of the parameters listed in the table and how the values used in the study were obtained:

- **Vehicle Engine Power**: The engine power was obtained from the vehicle specifications.

- **Engine Efficiency**: Power losses in the engine due to internal friction and other factors generally account for 5 to 10 percent of the engine losses for light-duty vehicles [18]. The losses were assumed to be 6 percent.

- **Vehicle Mass**: Vehicle mass is an important parameter in the model as it determines the force required to accelerate a vehicle. Vehicle weights were conducted using General

Electrodynamics Corporation (GEC) weigh scales with an advertised accuracy of 98 percent.

- **Percentage of Vehicle Mass on the Tractive Axle**: Each axle was weighed separately. In the case of light-duty vehicles, typical values for front-wheel drive vehicles are in the range of 50 to 65 percent, reflective of the high weight of the engine sitting on top of the axle. For rear-wheel drive vehicles, the mass on the tractive axle typically ranges between 35 to 50 percent of the total mass.

- **Frontal Area**: The frontal area of the vehicle was approximated as 85 percent of the height times the width of the vehicle (if the frontal area was not given directly in the vehicle specifications).

- **Air Drag Coefficient**: The air drag coefficient is given in the vehicle specifications. Typical values for light-duty vehicles range from 0.30 to 0.35, depending on the aerodynamic features of the vehicle. These values were also obtained from the vehicle specifications.

Table 1: Summary of Light-Duty Test Vehicle Characteristics

Vehicle	EPA Class	P (kW)	η	Mass (kg)	m_{ta}/m (%)	A (m²)	C_d	Throttle Level
1996 Geo Metro Hatchback	Subcompact	41.0	0 65	1130	0.380	1.88	0.34	83%
1995 Acura Integra SE		105.9	0 68	1670	0.515	1.94	0.32	89%
1995 Saturn SL	Compact	92.5	0.72	1240	0.560	1.95	0.33	84%
2001 Mazda Protégé LX 2.0		97.0	0.70	1610	0.525	2.04	0.34	92%
2001 Plymouth Neon		98.5	0.75	1650	0.495	2.07	0.36	87%
1998 Ford Taurus	Midsize	108.2	0 80	1970	0.575	2.26	0.30	88%
1998 Honda Accord		111.9	0.75	1770	0.610	2.12	0.34	57%
1995 BMW 740I		210.4	0.70	2370	0.515	2.27	0.32	85%
1995 Dodge Intrepid	Large	120.1	0 68	2040	0.535	2.30	0.31	66%
1999 Ford Crown Victoria		149.2	0.70	2300	0.590	2.44	0.34	80%
1998 Ford Windstar LX	Minivan	149.2	0 65	2270	0.550	2.73	0.40	59%
1995 Chevy S-10	Pickup	145.47	0.72	1930	0.605	2.31	0.45	55%
1995 Chevy Blazer	SUV	145.47	0 65	2310	0.560	2.49	0.45	63%

Data Collection Procedures

Each of the test vehicles was subjected to the same set of tests. The test runs involved accelerating the vehicles from a complete stop at the maximum acceleration rate over the entire length of the 1.6-km test section from 0 km/h to the maximum attainable speed within the test section. Depending on the type of vehicle, maximum speeds attained by the end of the test section for light-duty vehicles varied between 128 and 160 km/h (80 and 100 mph) and were much lower for the heavy-duty trucks. In conducting the study, a minimum of five repetitions were executed for each test set in order to provide a sufficient sample size for the validation analysis.

In each test run, the speed and position of the vehicle was recorded using a portable Global Positioning System (GPS) receiver connected to a laptop. Outputs from the GPS receiver included latitude, longitude, altitude, speed, heading, and time stamp once every second. Nominal position accuracy was specified with a 25-m (82-ft) spherical error probability, while nominal velocity accuracy was specified within 0.1 m/s (0.31 ft/s) error probability. Consequently, the error in acceleration estimates was within 0.1 m/s^2 given that they were computed every 2 seconds.

Roadway Parameters

To apply the vehicle dynamics model, five parameters linked to roadway characteristics must be determined: pavement type, pavement coefficient of friction, roadway grade, rolling coefficients, and altitude of roadway.

- **Pavement**: The pavement type and condition are required to determine several parameters. The selected test section on the Smart Road facility had a Pavement Serviceability Index greater than 3.0 and thus was classified as "good." The pavement condition affects the coefficient of friction and rolling coefficients, as described in detail by Rakha et al. [20]. Consequently, a coefficient of friction of 0.8 and values of 1.25, 0.0328, and 4.575 were selected for the coefficients C_r, c_5, and c_6, respectively.

- **Grade**: The roadway grade was computed using Equation (14) at each vehicle position.

- **Altitude**: This is the altitude above sea level for the testing location, in meters. Since the Smart Road sits at an altitude of 600m, this led to determination of an altitude coefficient of 0.95, as described by Rakha et al. [20].

Validation Results

Using the roadway and vehicle parameters, the proposed model was used to compute the evolution of the vehicle powertrain parameters over time. Given that the level of throttle input provided by the driver (human-in-the-loop) was unknown, this parameter was optimized to minimize the sum of squared error (E) between the model and the field-observed speed and position predictions as

$$E = \frac{\sqrt{\sum_{t=0}^{T}\left(\hat{v}_t - v_t\right)^2}}{\overline{v}} + \frac{\sqrt{\sum_{t=0}^{T}\left(\hat{x}_t - x_t\right)^2}}{\overline{x}} \tag{15}$$

where T is the total travel time (s), hat variables (^) are model-estimated parameters, and non-hat variables are field observations. The sum of squared error is normalized by dividing by the average field-observed speed and distance traveled in order to ensure that the error is dimensionless.

The optimum throttle level values that were estimated for the 13 test vehicles, which are summarized in Table 1, ranged from 55 to 92 percent with an average throttle level of 76 percent and a standard deviation of 14 percent. In capturing the vehicle behavior, Figure 3 demonstrates a quality match between the model estimates and field measurements. The various symbols in the figure reflect the different runs that were executed on the test facility. The first of the subplots in the figure illustrates the variation in the vehicle speed as a function of the travel time. This figure clearly demonstrates a quality match between the estimated and observed speed profiles. The second subplot compares the temporal variation in predicted vehicle acceleration levels against the field observations. Again, the figure clearly demonstrates an ideal match between field and simulated behavior. The third subplot demonstrates an excellent match between field-observed and model-estimated vehicle trajectories. The temporal variation in the transmission gear demonstrates that the vehicle travels in the first gear for approximately 8 seconds before upshifting to the second gear. The vehicle remains in the second gear for approximately 4 seconds before shifting to the third gear; finally, the vehicle shifts to the fourth gear after 32 seconds.

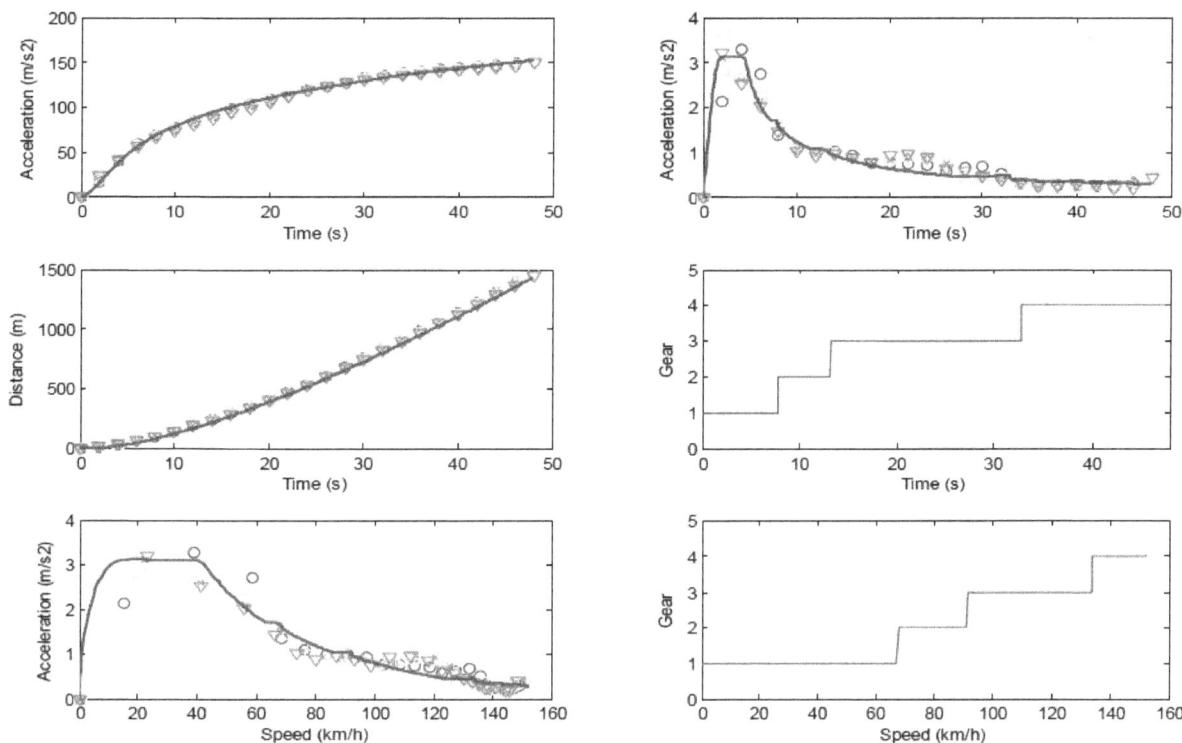

Figure 3: Model Validation against Field Measurements (Ford Crown Victoria)

Similar matches to the field data are observed for a compact vehicle (Mazda Protégé), as illustrated in Figure 4, and a midsized vehicle (BMW 740i), as illustrated in Figure 5. A comparison of the various vehicle behaviors demonstrates that larger vehicle engines are able to make gear shifts later in time and at higher speeds, while smaller engines require gear shifts at lower speeds.

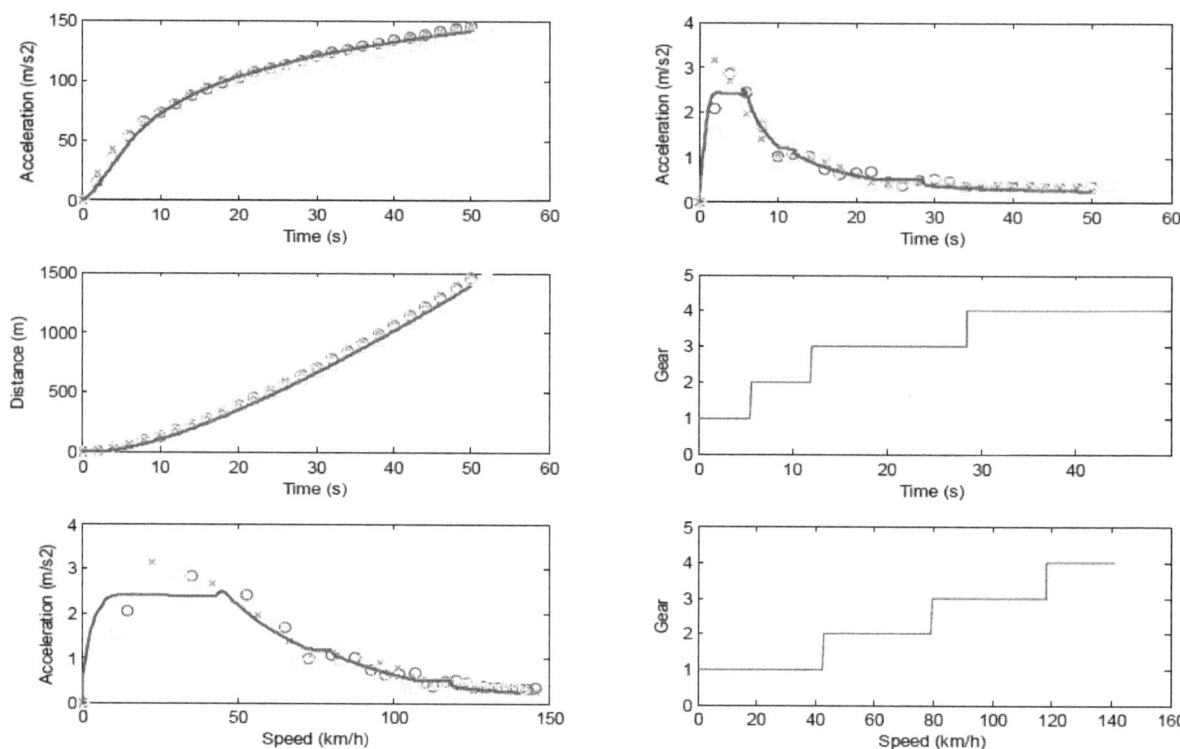

Figure 4: Model Validation against Field Measurements (Mazda Protégé)

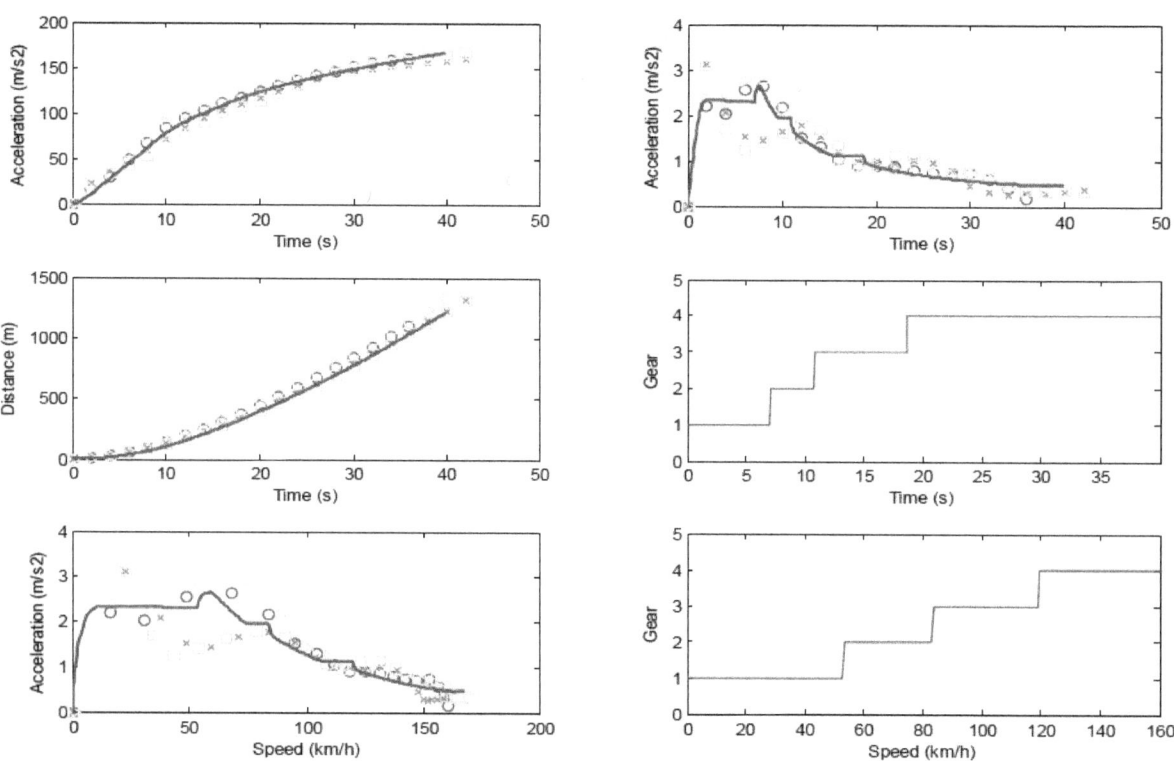

Figure 5: Model Validation against Field Measurements (BMW 740i)

1.3 Model Test II

The second validation of the proposed powertrain model was conducted comparing field data which were collected on Interstate 81. A 22-km section between mileposts 132 (Roanoke, VA) and 118 (Christiansburg, VA) which ranges from an elevation of 350 m to 629 m above mean sea level was selected. In the southbound direction, the maximum grade along the study section is 4 percent, and the maximum downhill grade is -5 percent with an average grade of 0.6 percent; more downhill grade sections are observed in the northbound direction. Both southbound and northbound trips were collected and analyzed for the study. The test vehicles' driving-related data were collected using an OBD II data logger.

Cruise control (CC) operation data were utilized for this validation section. The target speed was set to 104 km/h (or 65 mph). Figures 6, 7, and 8 illustrate the measured instantaneous vehicle power rate of the southbound and northbound sections of Interstate 81 and the estimated power from the proposed model. The results clearly demonstrate a good agreement between the instantaneous power estimates and field measurements. Three test vehicles (Chevy Malibu, Chevy Tahoe, and Toyota Camry) were utilized for the validation study. As illustrated in the figures, the predicted power generally follows the peaks and valleys of the measured data except for a few high power points. Specifically, the 2007 Chevy Malibu generated 13,297 kW of power along the southbound section of Interstate 81 while the proposed model estimated 13,871 kW of power using the same speed and road topographic profile, which is approximately 4.3 percent of error. Overall, the developed powertrain model estimated the vehicle power within reasonable accuracy. The model estimates instantaneous vehicle power within 1.7 to 20.2 percent error range when compared to the field measured power data for test vehicles.

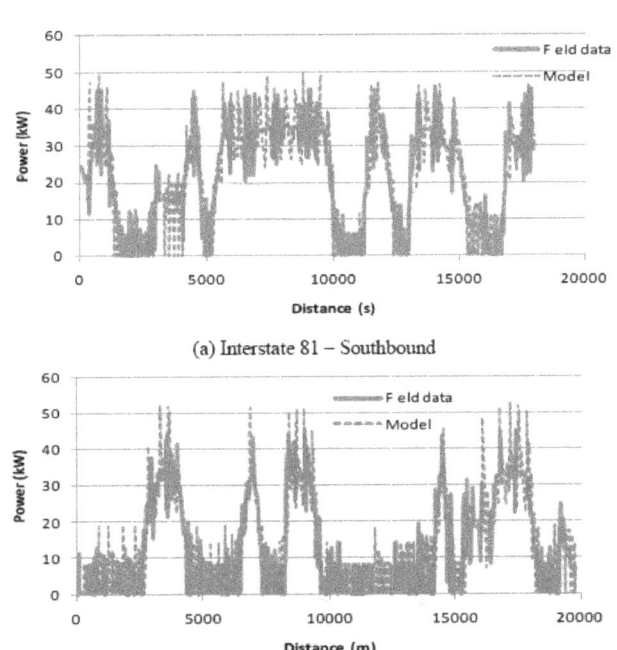

(a) Interstate 81 – Southbound

(b) Interstate 81 – Northbound

Figure 6: Instantaneous Model Validation (2007 Chevy Malibu)

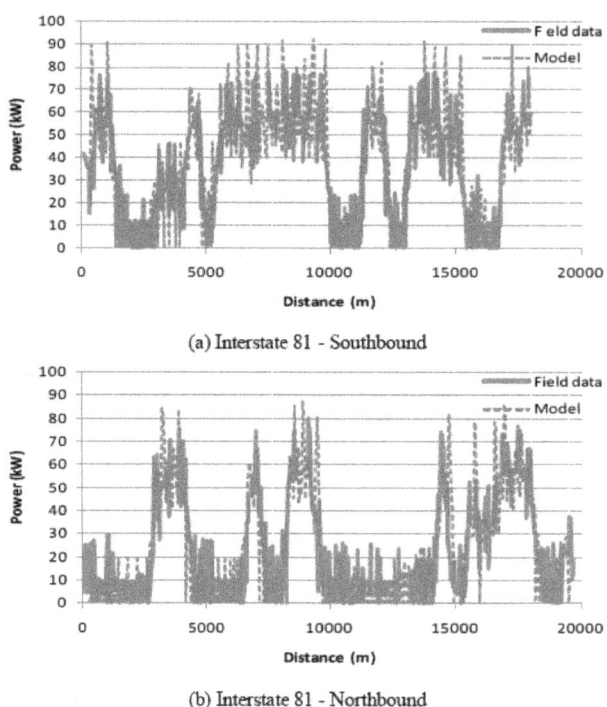

(a) Interstate 81 - Southbound

(b) Interstate 81 - Northbound

Figure 7: Instantaneous Model Validation (2008 Chevy Tahoe)

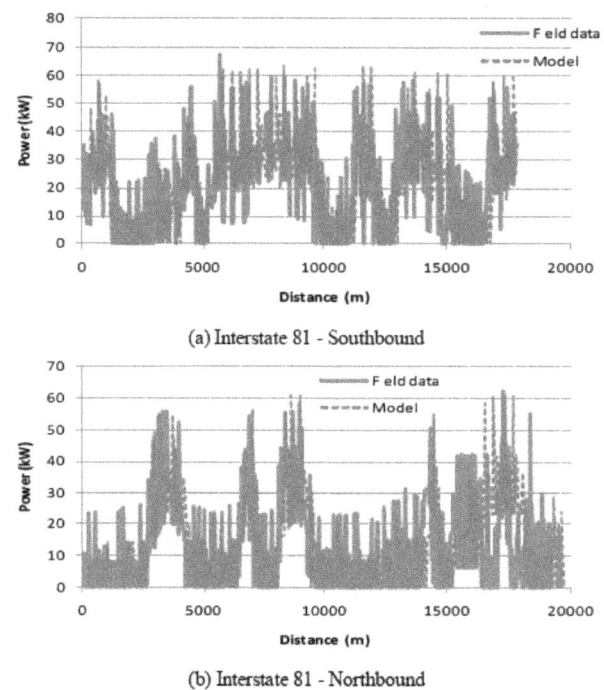

(a) Interstate 81 - Southbound

(b) Interstate 81 - Northbound

Figure 8: Instantaneous Model Validation (2011 Toyota Camry)

Figure 9 illustrates the power distributions of the model estimates and the field data for southbound and northbound sections of Interstate 81 trips for the Chevy Malibu test vehicle. The figures illustrate a good fit between the model estimates and the field measurements. Specifically, the predictions typically follow the power distribution trend for both southbound and northbound trips except for a few cases. As shown in the figures, the southbound trips (which involve uphill grade sections) require more vehicle power than the northbound trips.

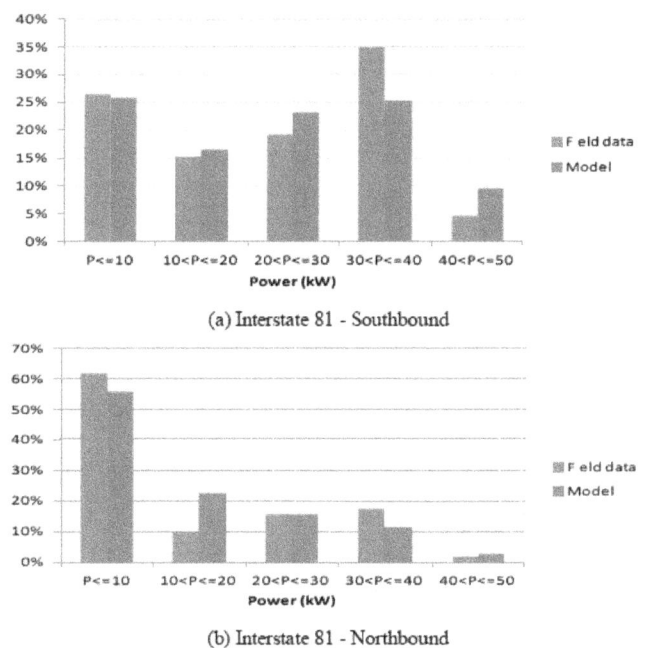

(a) Interstate 81 - Southbound

(b) Interstate 81 - Northbound

Figure 9: Power Distribution (2007 Chevy Malibu)

1.4 Conclusions

The research developed a simple vehicle powertrain model that can be integrated with car-following models within microscopic traffic simulation software. This simple model can be calibrated using engine and powertrain parameters that are publicly available without the need for field data collection. The model uses the driver throttle level input to: compute the engine speed; model the transmission system (manual and automatic); and compute the vehicle's acceleration, speed, position, and fuel consumption level. The model was demonstrated to produce vehicle acceleration, speed, position, and fuel consumption estimates that are consistent with field observations.

2. VIRGINIA TECH COMPREHENSIVE POWER-BASED FUEL CONSUMPTION MODEL: MODEL DEVELOPMENT AND VALIDATION

This section presents a new power-based microscopic fuel consumption model entitled the Virginia Tech Comprehensive Power-based Fuel Consumption Model (VT-CPFM). The transportation sector consumes approximately 30% of the total energy in the United States, which is mostly petroleum-based products including gasoline and diesel fuels. Significant emissions of CO_2, a GHG linked to climate change, are also attributed to the transportation sector. However, it would be difficult to imagine modern life without motorized transportation. Alternative transportation energy sources such as hybrid-electric technologies, bio-ethanol, and hydrogen fuel cells are emerging and are being broadly investigated as replacements for the conventional internal combustion engine. However, these new alternatives have not been able to replace petroleum-powered engines because of challenges that relate to availability, cost, convenience, lack of technology, and accessibility.

One of the key strategies for improving vehicle fuel efficiency is extracing more miles from each liter or gallon of fuel. A recent report estimated that teaching consumers to eco-drive can improve actual fuel efficiency by an average of 17% [21]. Eco-driving comprises driving behaviors that maximize fuel economy and correspondingly reduce GHG emissions. A simple, accurate, and efficient fuel consumption model is required to optimize the vehicle throttle and gear level in order to minimize the vehicle fuel consumption level over a future horizon (a predictive eco-cruise control [ECC] system).

This study develops and evaluates a new power-based microscopic fuel consumption model, VT-CPFM. The new model overcomes two main deficiencies of current models by addressing the following two issues: (a) the ability to produce a control system that does not result in bang-bang control [22], and (b) is easily calibrated using publicly available data. There are four major criteria to be considered for the proposed fuel consumption model: real-time computation, accuracy, model structure, and model calibration simplicity. First, the model must provide real-time computations instead of aggregated trip fuel consumption estimates. Second, the model should provide reasonable accuracy with the fewest input variables while not producing a bang-bang control strategy. Third, the model should be simple to reduce the computational load. Finally, the proposed model should be applicable for general vehicle populations, and should be calibrated using publicly available data. The proposed models that are presented in this paper satisfy all four criteria.

2.1 State-of-the-Art Microscopic Fuel Consumption Modeling Tools

Vehicle fuel consumption levels are typically derived from a relationship between instantaneous fuel consumption rates and instantaneous measurements of various explanatory variables including vehicle power, force (or tractive effort), acceleration, speed, and/or roadway grade. Numerous fuel consumption models have been developed that incorporate different explanatory variables in order to satisfy their specific objectives. One variable that stands out is vehicle power or vehicle-specific power (VSP), which is the power exerted per unit mass. Vehicle power can be computed as the product of the total force exerted by the vehicle and the vehicle velocity. The total force includes both the net force and the force that is required to overcome the aerodynamic, rolling, and grade resistance forces. Assuming that the vehicle fuel consumption rate is proportional to the vehicle power, the fuel consumption can be estimated by computing the forces acting on the vehicle.

Post et al. [23] developed a fuel consumption model that is a linear function of the instantaneous power demand. The model was built from chassis dynamometer experiments of 177 in-use vehicles [23]. This model was subsequently enhanced in later publications [24, 25]. The Comprehensive Modal Emissions Model (CMEM) is another model that estimates the instantaneous fuel consumption rate based on power, engine friction, engine speed, and vehicle engine size (or displacement) [26, 27]. Another fuel consumption model that makes use of topographic and gear shifting information was developed by researchers from Linköpings University [28-31].

While the majority of fuel consumption models were developed as power-demand models, the VT-Micro model was developed as a statistical model from experimentation with numerous polynomial combinations of speed and acceleration levels to construct a dual-regime model [32, 33].

Apart from the VT-Micro model, all models described in the literature produce a bang-bang type of control system. This occurs because the partial derivative of the fuel consumption rate with respect to the engine torque (T) is not a function of torque [22] or $\partial F/\partial T \neq f(T)$. A model that results in a bang-bang control system would indicate that the optimum fuel economy control would be to accelerate at full throttle in order to reduce the acceleration time. This type of control, which is obviously incorrect, would recommend that the driver drive as aggressively as possible in order to minimize the fuel consumption level.

In addition, all existing models require the calibration of their parameters by collecting vehicle-specific in-laboratory or field data. This exercise is time-consuming, expensive, and does require vehicle instrumentation to gather the required data. The proposed model attempts to address these two deficiencies in existing models, namely: the ability to result in a non-bang-bang control and the ability to calibrate the model parameters using publicly available fuel consumption and vehicle driveline data. The proposed modeling framework is described in the following section.

2.2 Proposed Comprehensive Fuel Consumption Modeling Framework

Vehicle fuel consumption depends on many factors that may not be captured easily by a single mathematical model. Some of the factors include: engine design, vehicle age, driver behavior, road topography, fuel properties, resistive forces on the vehicle, ignition technology, cylinder head design, friction inside the engine, temperature, humidity level, and many other factors [34]. Compromising between simplicity and accuracy has always been a difficult task for any modeler so the challenge is to identify the key parameters for consideration in a model without creating a complicated model that poses a major calibration challenge.

One of the popular fuel consumption models that is presented in the mechanical engineering literature [34] is formulated in Equation (16), where the vehicle power is computed using Equation (17).

$$FC(t) = \mu\left(\frac{k\omega_e(t)d}{2000} + P(t)\right) \tag{16}$$

$$P(t) = \left(\frac{R(t) + ma(t)\left(1.04 + 0.0025\xi(t)^2\right)}{3600\eta_d} \cdot v(t)\right) \tag{17}$$

Here $FC(t)$ is the fuel consumption rate (l/s) at time t; μ is the specific fuel consumption (kg/kJ/s), which varies with the engine condition; k is the engine friction in kilopascals (kPa);

$\omega_e(t)$ is the engine speed in revolutions per second (rev/s) at time t; d is the engine displacement (l); and $P(t)$ is the total power exerted by the vehicle driveline (kW) at time t and is computed using Equation (17), where $R(t)$ is the total resistance force (N), m is the vehicle mass (kg), $a(t)$ is the vehicle acceleration (m/s^2) at time t, $v(t)$ is the vehicle speed (km/h) at time t; ζ is the gear ratio at time t, and η_d is the driveline efficiency. This model, however, produces a bang-bang control system as was demonstrated earlier.

Engine friction (k) is generally proportional to the engine speed during a trip [35]. However, it is difficult to obtain a relationship between engine friction (k) and engine speed for most vehicles without assistance from vehicle manufacturers. Consequently, it is typically assumed to be constant. The resistance force on the vehicle is computed as the sum of the aerodynamic, rolling, and grade resistance forces. The typical values of vehicle coefficients are provided in the literature [20].

The specific fuel consumption, which is the amount of fuel used per power unit produced, is typically observed from an engine performance graph, which is vehicle-specific [36]. In general, the specific fuel consumption varies as a function of the engine speed and has a parabolic shape. As engine speed increases, the specific fuel consumption rate decreases to a minimum value at engine speeds ranging between 2,000 to 3,500 rpm depending on the engine load, and then increases again for higher engine speeds. This is because the engine is developed to produce its best performance and highest efficiency in the 2,000 to 3,500 rpm range. In addition, engine friction loss is significantly higher at high engine speeds, causing an increase in the specific fuel consumption rate. The specific fuel consumption rate is also related to vehicle throttle levels. In the real world, vehicles do not typically operate at full engine load, but frequently change the throttle level. Even though the specific fuel consumption is a good concept to consider in the estimation of the fuel consumption rate, it is extremely difficult to measure. The data that were gathered using an OBD reader demonstrate that, for positive power conditions, the fuel consumption function is convex and could be modeled using a second-order polynomial model.

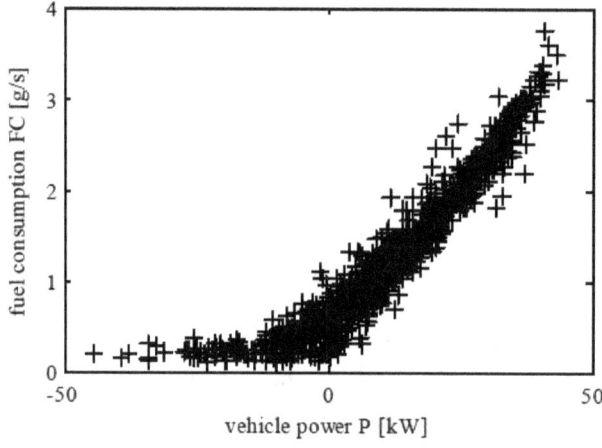

Figure 10: Typical Power vs. Fuel Consumption Functional Form

Consequently, two power-based second-order polynomial models are proposed in this paper. These models are entitled the Virginia Tech Comprehensive Power-based Fuel Consumption Model-1 and -2 (VT-CPFM-1 and VT-CPFM-2). The use of a second-order model with a positive second-order parameter is required in order to ensure that a bang-bang control does not result from the application of the model, as was described earlier in the paper. Addition of higher than second-order parameters would add to the complexity of the model and thus not allow for model calibration using the EPA city and highway cycles. Consequently, a second-order model provides a good compromise between model accuracy and applicability.

The two VT-CPFM models are formulated as

$$FC(t) = \begin{cases} \alpha_0 + \alpha_1 P(t) + \alpha_2 P(t)^2 & \forall\, P(t) \geq 0 \\ \alpha_0 & \forall\, P(t) < 0 \end{cases}, \text{ and} \tag{18}$$

$$FC(t) = \begin{cases} \beta_0 \omega_e(t) + \beta_1 P(t) + \beta_2 P(t)^2 & \forall\, P(t) \geq 0 \\ \beta_0 \omega_{idle} & \forall\, P(t) < 0 \end{cases}. \tag{19}$$

Where α_0, α_1, α_2 and β_0, β_1, and β_2 are vehicle-specific model constants that are calibrated for each vehicle and ω_{idle} is the engine idling speed (rpm). In the case of the VT-CPFM-1 model the power exerted at any instant t is computed using Equation (20).

$$P(t) = \left(\frac{R(t) + 1.04ma(t)}{3600\eta_d} \right) v(t). \tag{20}$$

The first model does not require any engine data given that the power exerted by a vehicle is a function of the vehicle speed and acceleration level, which can be measured directly using non-engine instrumentation such as, for example, a GPS. This model is ideal for implementation within microscopic traffic simulation software. This model, however, cannot be used to develop predictive eco-gear-shifting strategies given that changes in a vehicle's gear that results in changes in the engine speed would not be reflected in the fuel consumption estimates. The second model requires engine data in addition to external data and thus can be used to model eco-gear-shifting strategies but does require the explicit modeling of the vehicle driveline. Each of these models is described in detail in the following sections.

2.2.1 VT-CPFM-1 Model

As was mentioned earlier, the first model does not require engine data to estimate vehicle fuel consumption rates. The idling fuel consumption rate for the VT-CPFM-1 model is estimated using Equation (21) and bounded based on Equation (22) to ensure that the functional form is convex, as will be discussed later in the paper. The idling fuel consumption rate in Equation (21) is an average operating point method that was proposed by Guzzella and Sciarretta [14]. It should be noted that, in reality, the idling fuel consumption rate constantly fluctuates; however, the proposed model assumes, for simplicity purposes, that the rate remains constant.

$$\alpha_0 = \frac{P_{mfo}\,\omega_{idle}\,d}{22164 \times QN}. \tag{21}$$

$$\alpha_0 = \left[\frac{F_{city} - F_{hwy}\dfrac{P_{city}^2}{P_{hwy}^2}}{T_{city} - T_{hwy}\dfrac{P_{city}^2}{P_{hwy}^2}}, \; \frac{F_{city} - F_{hwy}\dfrac{P_{city}}{P_{city}} - \varepsilon\left(P_{city}^2 - P_{hwy}^2\dfrac{P_{city}}{P_{hwy}} \right)}{T_{city} - T_{hwy}\dfrac{P_{city}}{P_{city}}} \right] \tag{22}$$

Here P_{mfo} is the idling fuel mean pressure (400,000 Pa); ω_{idle} is the idling engine speed (rpm); d is the engine displacement (liters); Q is the fuel lower heating value (43,000,000 J/kg for gasoline fuel); N is the number of engine cylinders; F_{city} and F_{hwy} are the total fuel consumed for the EPA city and highway drive cycles (liters), respectively (computed using Equations (23) and

(24), respectively); T_{city} and T_{hwy} are the durations of the city and highway cycles (1875s and 766s, respectively); and P_{city} and P^2_{city} are computed as the sum of power and power squared exerted each second over the entire cycle (computed using Equations (25) and (26), respectively). Similarly, P_{hwy} and P^2_{hwy} are estimated in the same manner for the highway cycle (computed using Equations (25) and (26), respectively). The ε term ensures that the second-order parameter (α_2) is greater than zero. Experimentation with the model revealed that a minimum value of 1E-06 ensures that the optimum fuel economy cruising speed is in the 60 to 80 km/h range which is typical of light-duty vehicles.

$$F_{city} = \frac{3.7854 \times 17.663}{1.6093 \times FE_{city}} = \frac{41.5546}{FE_{city}} \tag{23}$$

$$F_{hwy} = \frac{3.7854 \times 16.4107}{1.6093 \times FE_{hwy}} = \frac{38.6013}{FE_{hwy}} \tag{24}$$

$$P_{city} = \sum_{t=0}^{T_{city}} P(t) \text{ and } P_{hwy} = \sum_{t=0}^{T_{hwy}} P(t) \tag{25}$$

$$P^2_{city} = \sum_{t=0}^{T_{city}} P(t)^2 \text{ and } P^2_{hwy} = \sum_{t=0}^{T_{hwy}} P(t)^2 \tag{26}$$

It should be noted that the EPA started the use of additional drive cycles in 2008. These new tests—they had, in fact, been in use since the late 1990s but for emissions purposes only—are the US06 high-speed (80 mph max) cycle; the SC03, or "A/C," cycle, which is very similar to the city cycle but runs in 95-degree heat with the vehicle's air conditioning active; and the cold FTP test, which is exactly the same as the city cycle but runs at a temperature of 20°C. Until the 2012 model year, automakers ran the tests on the old drive cycles but reported the fuel-economy ratings for the new cycles using Equations (27) and (28) developed by the EPA. Here FE_{city} and FE_{hwy} are the fuel economy estimates for the old cycles while FE'_{city} and FE'_{hwy} are the estimates for the new drive cycles. It should be noted that the units of FE are in mi/gal in the case of U.S. cycles.

$$FE'_{city} = \frac{1}{\dfrac{1.18053}{FE_{city}} + 0.003259} \tag{27}$$

$$FE'_{hwy} = \frac{1}{\dfrac{1.3466}{FE_{hwy}} + 0.001376} \tag{28}$$

In order to ensure that the fuel consumption versus vehicle power relationship is convex, as illustrated in Figure 10, a constraint is introduced. Specifically, this constraint ensures that α_2 is positive and the α_1 can then be computed, as demonstrated in Equations (29) and (30). The parameter α_2 has to be greater than zero in order to ensure that the model does not produce a bang-bang control [22].

$$\alpha_1 = \frac{F_{hwy} - T_{hwy}\alpha_0 - P^2_{hwy}\alpha_2}{P_{hwy}} \tag{29}$$

$$\alpha_2 = \frac{\left(F_{city} - F_{hwy}\dfrac{P_{city}}{P_{hwy}}\right) - \left(T_{city} - T_{hwy}\dfrac{P_{city}}{P_{hwy}}\right)\alpha_0}{P_{city}^2 - P_{hwy}^2\dfrac{P_{city}}{P_{hwy}}} \geq \varepsilon = 10\text{E-06} \tag{30}$$

Once α_0 is computed, the remaining two model coefficients (α_1, α_2) can be estimated using the fuel economy ratings for the EPA city and highway drive cycles. As shown in Equation (31), the two variables α_1 and α_2 can be computed by solving a system of two linear equations as

$$\begin{aligned} F_{city} &= T_{city}\alpha_0 + P_{city}\alpha_1 + P_{city}^2\alpha_2 \\ F_{hwy} &= T_{hwy}\alpha_0 + P_{hwy}\alpha_1 + P_{hwy}^2\alpha_2 \end{aligned} \tag{31}$$

A MATLAB code has been developed that allows the user to input various vehicle parameters to calibrate the model coefficients, as illustrated in Figure 11. The user has the ability to input both U.S. and European fuel economy ratings. In the case of the U.S. drive cycles the standard city and highway cycles are used with the adjustments derived in Equations (32) and (33) for 2008 and later model years.

$$FE_{city} = \frac{1.18053}{\dfrac{1}{FE'_{city}} - 0.003259} \tag{32}$$

$$FE_{hwy} = \frac{1.3466}{\dfrac{1}{FE'_{hwy}} - 0.001376} \tag{33}$$

In the case of European vehicles the European drive cycles are used. The New European Drive Cycle (NEDC) is a driving cycle consisting of four repeated ECE-15 driving cycles and an Extra-Urban driving cycle, or EUDC. The NEDC attempts to represent the typical usage of a vehicle in Europe and is used, among other things, to assess the emission levels of car engines. It should be noted that in the case of the European cycles the fuel ratings are reported in liters per 100 km.

Figure 11 and Table 2 show the input parameters for a 2010 Honda Accord vehicle. The data include parameters for the estimation of the various resistance forces in addition to gear data that are used for the VT-CPFM-2 model in order to compute the engine speed as a function of the vehicle speed and engaged gear. It should be noted that the data values and sources are summarized in Table 2. Some model parameters may be assumed, as will be described. The engine efficiency accounts for the power losses in the engine due to internal friction and other factors. The engine efficiency factor ranges between 15 and 5% for light- and heavy-duty vehicles. The frontal area of the vehicle can be approximated as 85% of the vehicle height multiplied by its width if it is not given directly in the vehicle specifications. The air drag coefficient is typically provided on auto manufacturer websites; however, if this parameter is not available, typical values for light-duty vehicles range from 0.30 to 0.35, depending on the aerodynamic features of the vehicle. Heavy-duty vehicles have much higher drag coefficients ranging from 0.58 to 0.78. The tire size for a Honda Accord is reported as P215/60 R16 on the Honda website. The 215 parameter is the tire width in millimeters, measured from the bottom of the bead to the bottom of the bead; the 60 is the sidewall aspect ratio, the ratio of sidewall height to tire width at the tread (indicating that the sidewall height is 60% of the tread width); and the 16 is the wheel rim diameter in inches. Consequently, in this example, the tire radius is computed as 33.22 cm ($21.5 \times 0.6 + 16 \times 2.54 / 2$).

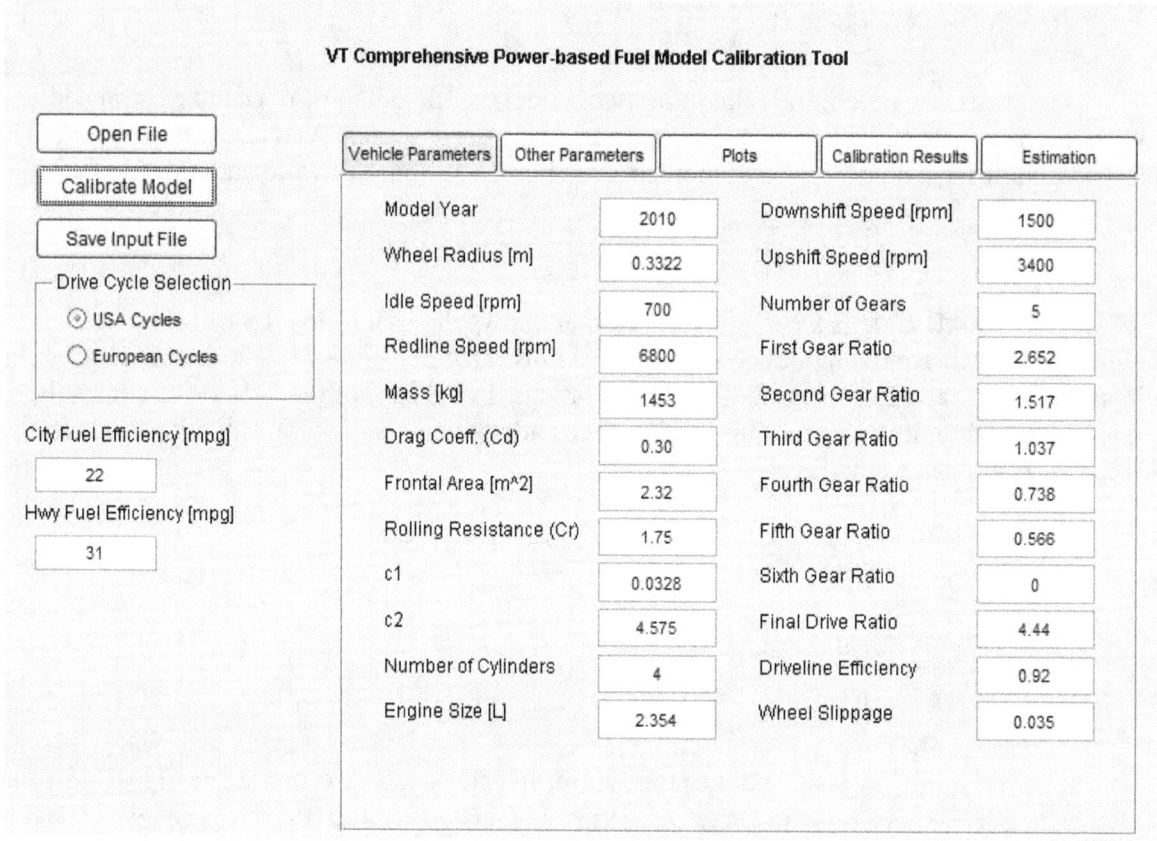

Figure 11: Illustration of VT-CPFM Calibration Tool

Table 2: List of Parameters Required for Model Calibration

Parameter	Required for VT-CPFM-1?	Required for VT-CPFM-2?	Value	Source
Model Year	Yes	Yes		Auto website
Wheel Radius	No	Yes		Auto website
Idling Speed	No	Yes	600-750 rpm	Auto website
Redline Speed	No	Yes		Auto website
Downshift Speed	No	Yes	1500 rpm	Field data
Upshift Speed	No	Yes	3400 rpm	Field data
Vehicle Mass [kg]	Yes	Yes		Auto website
Drag Coeff (C_D)	Yes	Yes		Auto website
Frontal Area (A_f)	Yes	Yes	0.85x heightxwidth	Auto website
Rolling Coefficient (C_r)	Yes	Yes	1.75	[20]
c_1	Yes	Yes	0.0328	[20]
c_2	Yes	Yes	4.575	[20]
Driveline Efficiency	Yes	Yes	85 to 95%	[20]
Wheel Slippage	Yes	Yes	2 to 5%	[34]
Number of Cylinders	Yes	Yes		Auto website
Engine Size [L]	Yes	Yes		Auto website
Number of Gears	No	Yes		Auto website
Various Gear Ratios	No	Yes		Auto website
Final Drive Ratio	No	Yes		Auto website
Altitude [m]	Yes	Yes		GPS receiver
P_{mfo} [Pa]	Yes	Yes	400000	[18]
Q [J/kg]	Yes	Yes	43000000	[18]

2.2.2. VT-CPFM-2 Model

The VT-CPFM-2 model that was presented earlier in Equation (19) can be calibrated in a similar fashion. The engine speed coefficient is computed as

$$\beta_0 = \frac{P_{mfo}d}{22164 \times QN}. \tag{34}$$

The two remaining parameters can then be calibrated using the EPA fuel economy ratings for the city and highway cycles using Equations (35) and (36).

$$\beta_1 = \frac{\left(\frac{F_{city} - \omega_{city}\beta_0 - P_{city}^2\beta_2}{P_{city}} \right) + \left(\frac{F_{hwy} - \omega_{hwy}\beta_0 - P_{hwy}^2\beta_2}{P_{hwy}} \right)}{2} \tag{35}$$

$$\beta_2 = \frac{\left(F_{city} - F_{hwy}\frac{P_{city}}{P_{hwy}} \right) - \left(\omega_{city} - \omega_{hwy}\frac{P_{city}}{P_{hwy}} \right)\beta_0}{P_{city}^2 - P_{hwy}^2\frac{P_{city}}{P_{hwy}}} \geq 1E\text{-}06 \tag{36}$$

All terms are similar to the earlier definitions except for the ω_{city} and ω_{hwy} parameters that are computed using Equations (37) and (38).

$$\omega_{city} = \sum_{t=0}^{T_{city}} \omega(t) \tag{37}$$

$$\omega_{hwy} = \sum_{t=0}^{T_{hwy}} \omega(t) \tag{38}$$

Again, the MATLAB code provides an automated tool for the calibration of the model parameters for both North American and European vehicles.

2.3 Model Validation

The validation of the proposed fuel consumption models was conducted considering validation of instantaneous fuel consumption measurements, validation of trip fuel consumption estimates, and validation of optimum cruise speeds. This section presents the results of the various validation efforts.

2.3.1. Validation of Instantaneous Fuel Consumption Estimates

For validation purposes, the model was calibrated to three vehicles using the procedures described in the previous section. The three vehicles included a Ford Explorer (4.0L, 2,223 kg), a Saturn SL (1.9L, 1,240 kg), and a Honda Accord (2.2L, 1,605 kg). These vehicles were selected to include a light-duty truck (Ford Explorer) and two light-duty passenger cars. The vehicles were run on three drive cycles on a chassis dynamometer: the arterial level of service (LOS) A cycle, the LA92 cycle, and the New York cycle. These three cycles were selected for validation purposes because they represent a wide range of real-world driving conditions. The arterial LOS A (ARTA) drive cycle involves several full and partial stops in addition to travel at a fairly high speed (in the range of 100 km/h), representing the normal driving conditions of arterial and/or collector roads. The LA92 cycle, often called the unified driving schedule, was developed as an emission inventory improvement tool by the California Air Resources Board (CARB). Compared to the FTP, the LA92 has a greater top speed, a greater average speed, less idle time, fewer stops per distance, and a greater acceleration level. Finally, the New York cycle features low-speed, stop-and-go traffic conditions and involves more aggressive and realistic driving behavior for congested urban areas.

The instantaneous measured and estimated fuel consumption rates were compared by running the test vehicles on the three drive cycles, as illustrated in Figure 12 and Figure 13. Superimposed on the figures are the VT-CPFM-1 model estimates, which were computed using each of the vehicle-specific parameters. In order to capture the temporal autocorrelation in fuel consumption levels, an exponential smoothing filter was applied. The smoothing process combines α % (smoothing parameter) of the newly estimated instantaneous fuel consumption level from the VT-CPFM model with (1-α) % of the fuel consumption of the previously smoothed estimate. The smoothing parameter was optimized by minimizing the sum of squared error between estimated and field-measured fuel consumption levels. In the case of the Honda Accord and Saturn SL test vehicles, the optimum smoothing factor was 45%; and it was 15% for the Ford Explorer. Based on experimentation with various vehicles, a smoothing factor of 20% was found to provide a level of autocorrelation consistent with field observations.

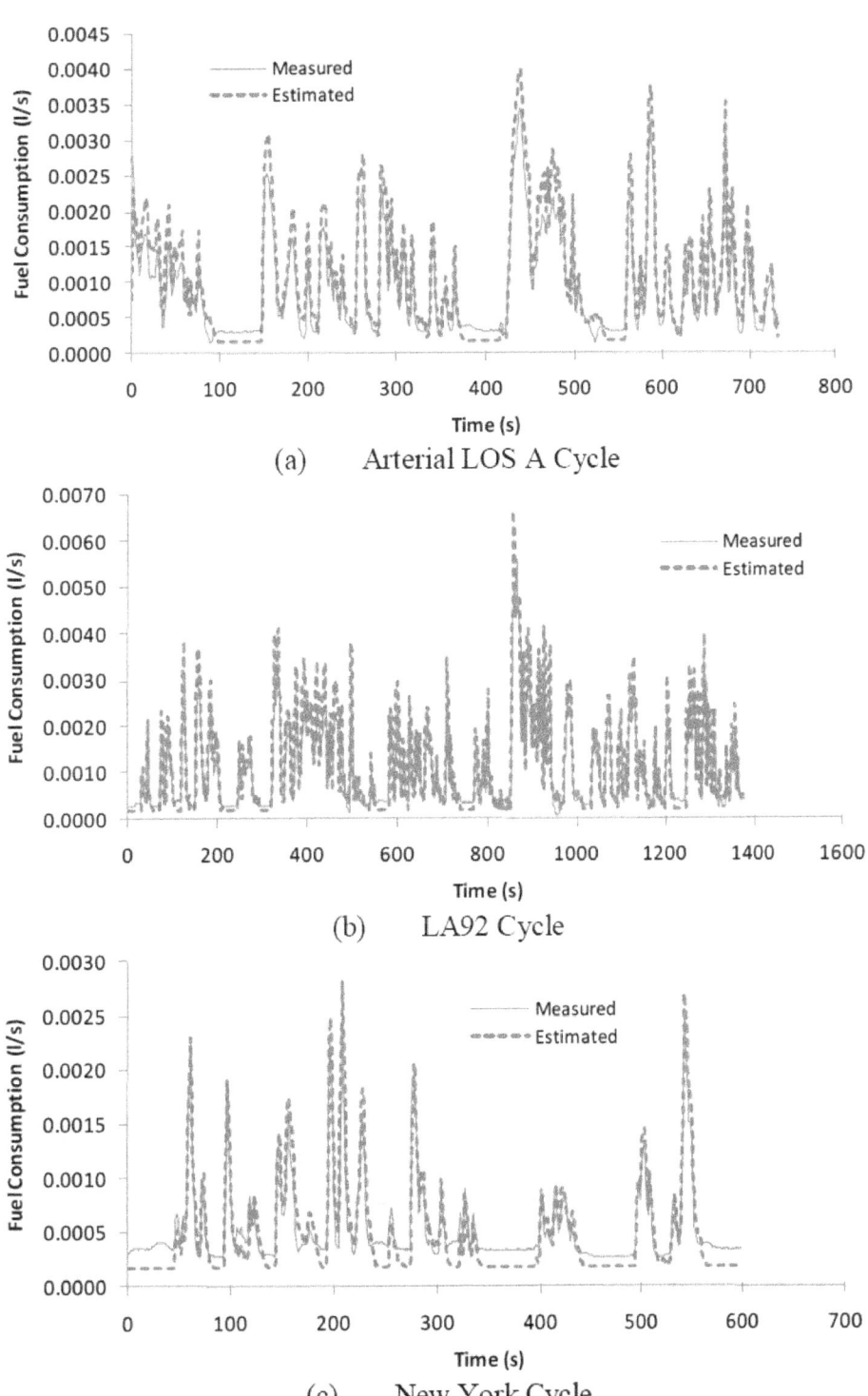

(a)   Arterial LOS A Cycle

(b)   LA92 Cycle

(c)   New York Cycle

Figure 12: Instantaneous Model Validation, Honda Accord

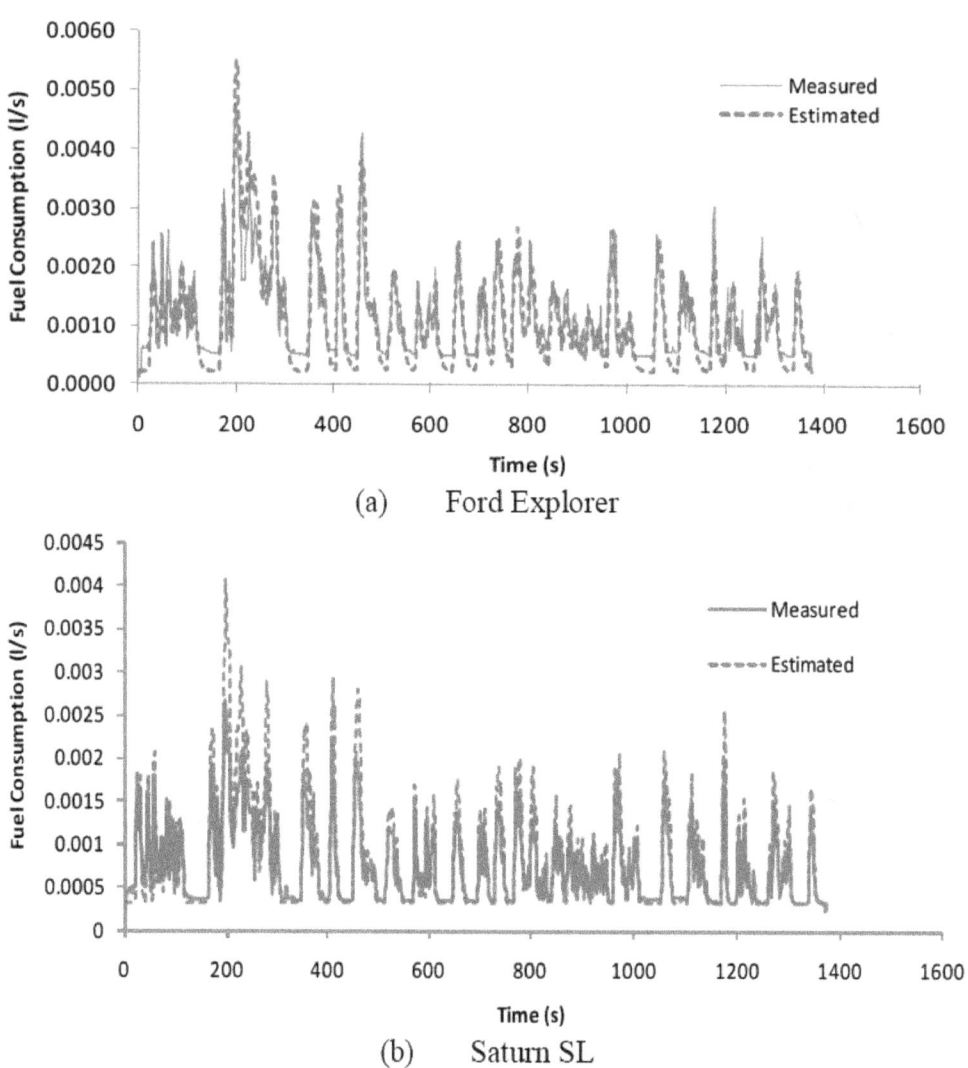

(a)   Ford Explorer

(b)   Saturn SL

Figure 13: Instantaneous Model Validation, City Cycle

As illustrated in Figure 12 and Figure 13, the predicted fuel consumption rates generally follow the peaks and valleys of the measured data and demonstrate a good agreement with field measurements. While it appears that the proposed model slightly overestimates some fuel consumption rates for the City cycle, in general, the model predictions follow the field-collected fuel measurements with high correlation coefficients (94% to 98%), as illustrated in Figure 14. Specifically, in the case of the New York cycle, in which a line slope of 1.0 indicates a close match between predicted and measured fuel consumption levels, the figure illustrates that the slopes of the lines are between from 93% to 98%.

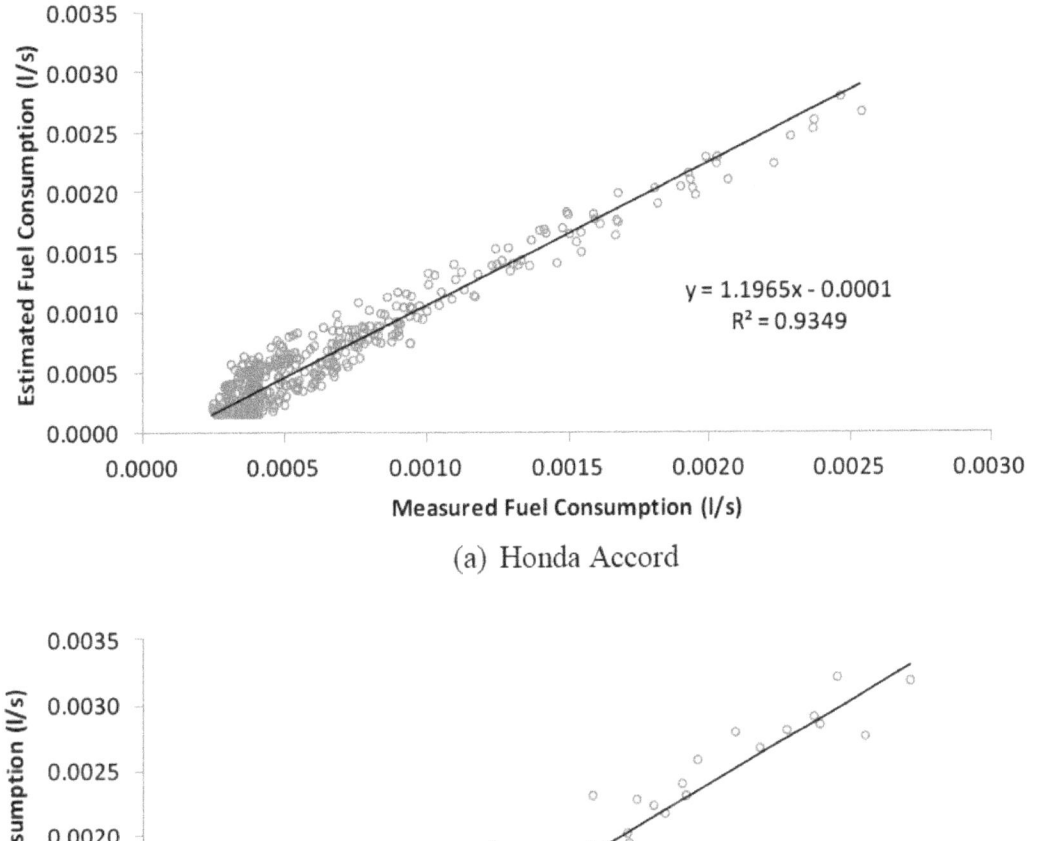

(a) Honda Accord

(b) Saturn SL

Figure 14: Instantaneous model validation, New York Cycle

2.3.2. Trip Level Validation

In order to evaluate the accuracy of the proposed model, model estimates were compared to field-collected fuel consumption data. The field measurements were gathered by the EPA. The validation effort involved an aggregated trip level comparison over 16 drive cycles using three test vehicles that were utilized for the instantaneous model validation, as illustrated in Figure 15. The database includes many off-cycle (non-FTP) fuel data over different facility types and therefore provides a good assessment of the quality of model estimates for different roadway types and different levels of congestion.

Figure 15 illustrates the model estimates and two EPA's field data for different driving cycles. One data set (measured 1) represents the fuel consumption data under FTP ambient conditions using the standard vehicle certification test fuel. The second data set (measured 2) represents extreme conditions that consume more fuel than normal driving conditions. In addition, the red bars illustrate the proposed model's fuel economy estimates using the three test vehicles. The figure clearly illustrates a good fit between the model estimates and the field measurements. Specifically, the predictions typically lay within the two field measurements (except for a few cases). Furthermore, the model estimates generally follow the average field data of the test vehicle's fuel economy under different driving conditions. Furthermore, it is noted that Fwy AC, High Speed, and Hwy D cycles generate good fuel economy trips while the fuel economy values of ART E and New York cycles are relatively lower than the other trip cycles.

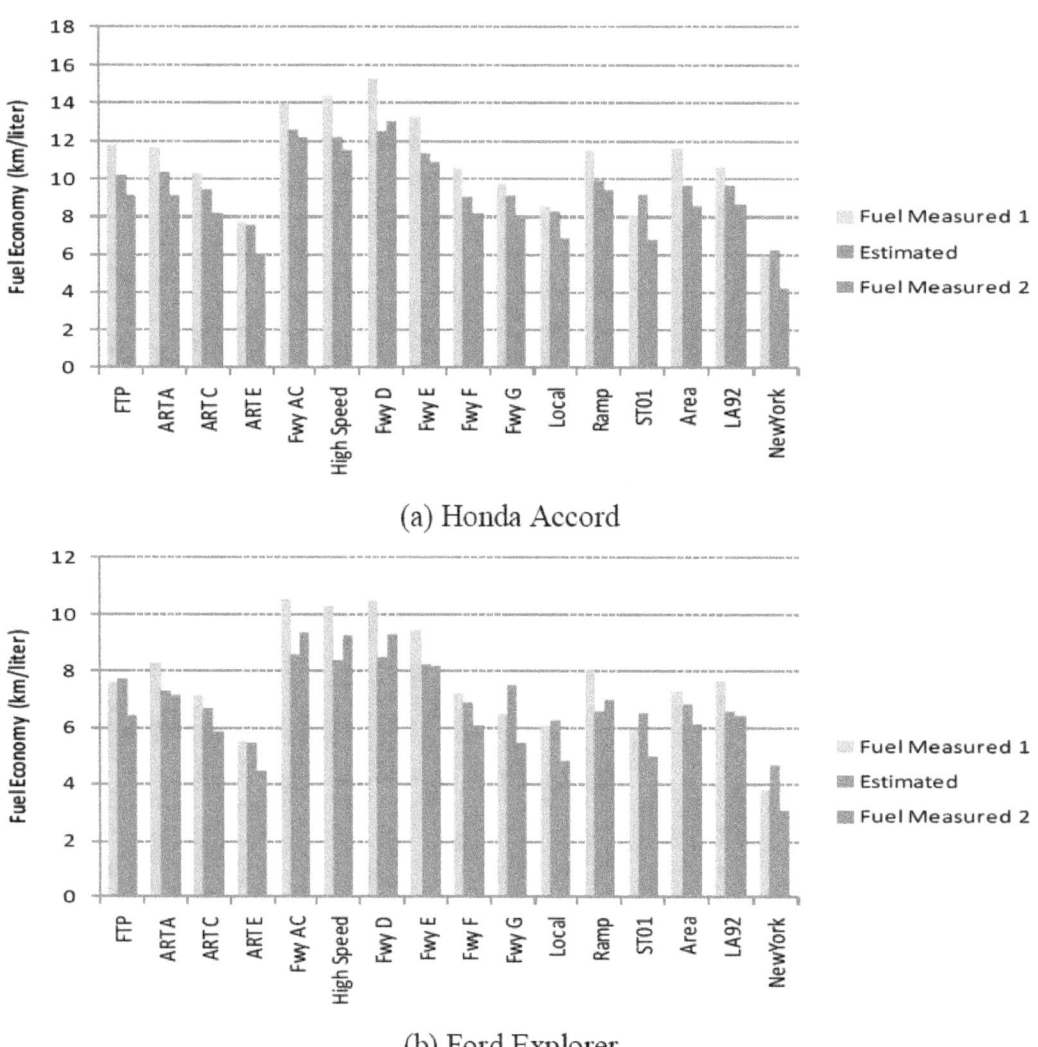

(a) Honda Accord

(b) Ford Explorer

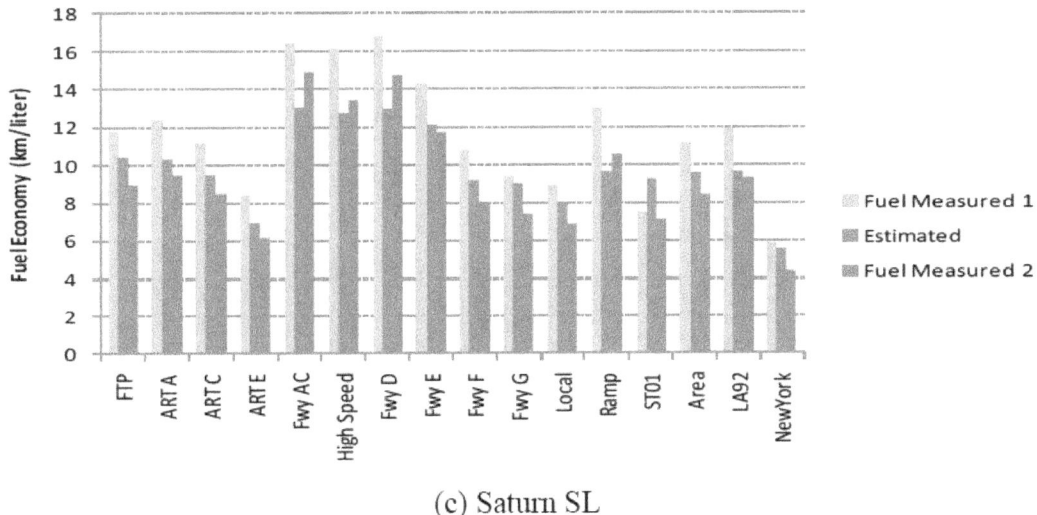

(c) Saturn SL

Figure 15: Simulated Fuel Economy for Different Driving Cycles

2.3.3. Optimum Cruise Speed Validation

The next validation effort established the validity of the model predictions of the optimum cruise speeds. In validating the model, a comparison was made to the VT-Micro model estimates for the Oak Ridge National Laboratory (ORNL) average vehicle. The ORNL test vehicles were driven in the field in order to verify their maximum operating boundary. Subsequently, vehicle fuel consumption and emission rates were measured in a laboratory on a chassis dynamometer within the vehicle's feasible vehicle speed and acceleration envelope. Data sets were generated that included vehicle energy consumption and emission rates as a function of the vehicle's instantaneous speed and acceleration levels. Several measurements were made in order to obtain an average fuel consumption and emission rate [37]. The eight normal-emitting vehicles included five light-duty automobiles and three light-duty trucks. These vehicles were selected in order to produce an average vehicle that was consistent with average vehicle sales in terms of engine displacement, vehicle curb weight, and vehicle type [37]. Specifically, the average engine size was 3.3 L, the average number of cylinders was 5.8, and the average curb weight was 1497 kg (3300 lbs). Industry reports show that the average sales-weighted domestic engine size in 1995 was 3.5 L, with an average of 5.8 cylinders.

As illustrated in Figure 16, the VT-CPFM-1 and VT-CPFM-2 models are consistent with the VT-Micro predictions of optimum cruise speeds and produce the same bowl-shaped curve as a function of vehicle cruise speed. Specifically, the optimum speed ranges between 60 and 80 km/h for the two test vehicles (2010 Honda Civic and 2010 Honda Accord). It should be noted that the VT-CPFM fuel consumption estimates are lower because the vehicles that were modeled are newer and, thus, are more efficient vehicles.

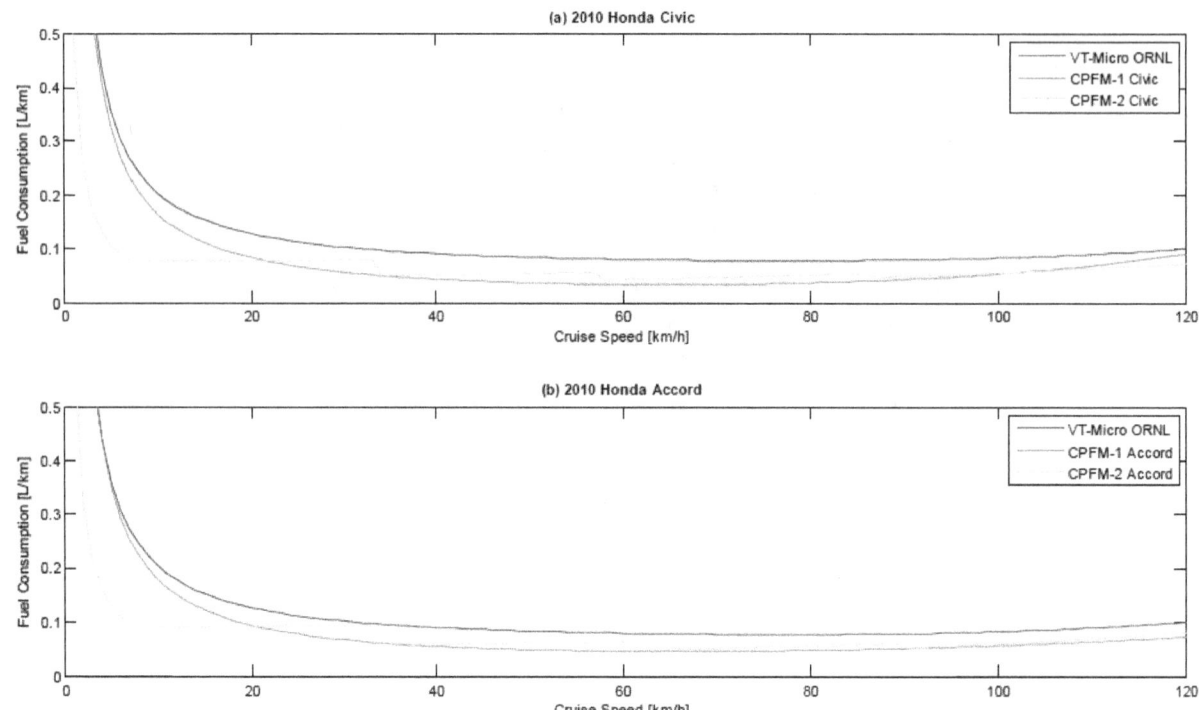

Figure 16: Impact of Cruise Speed of Vehicle Consumption Rate

2.4 Estimation of CO$_2$ Emissions

CO$_2$ emissions are directly associated with fuel consumption rates. As demonstrated in Equation (13), CO$_2$ emissions can be estimated from the carbon balance equation using fuel consumption and HC and CO emissions. Since the absolute value of CO$_2$ emissions is significantly higher than HC and CO emissions, the prediction of CO$_2$ emissions is primarily affected by the fuel consumption level. In an attempt to calibrate the CO$_2$ emission rate, a Ford Crown Victoria test vehicle was tested using on-board emission measurement (OEM) equipment. The data were collected from the Route 460 Bypass between Christiansburg and Blacksburg, Virginia. The field data collection involved running the test vehicle at a constant speed (104 km/h) along the Route 460 Bypass. The test vehicle was accelerated from a complete stop and continued to accelerate until the vehicle reached a speed of 104 km/h at a normal acceleration level and decelerated to a complete stop. A total of 11 valid trip repetitions were made in order to ensure that sufficient data were available. Equation (39) was utilized to estimate the CO$_2$ emission level for all 11 trips. It is interesting to note that the value of the estimated parameter is almost identical to the value derived from the carbon balance equation without HC and CO emissions. The θ parameter was found to be 2330 when CO$_2$ emissions are in g/s and fuel consumption estimates are in l/s.

$$\theta = \frac{\sum_{t=0}^{T} CO_2(t)}{\sum_{t=0}^{T} F(t)} \tag{39}$$

Two different data sets were employed in Figure 17 to compare the measured CO$_2$ emissions to the estimated CO$_2$ emissions. The data from Figure 17(a) are the data that were collected along Route 460, and the second data set was collected on a dynamometer by the EPA along the LA04 cycle, also known as the city cycle. The figure demonstrates good agreement between the predicted and measured CO_2 emissions. Specifically, the proposed model estimated the CO_2 emissions within a 2% error range, and the coefficients of correlation of the two examples were measured at up to 99% along the Route 460 trips and LA04 cycle.

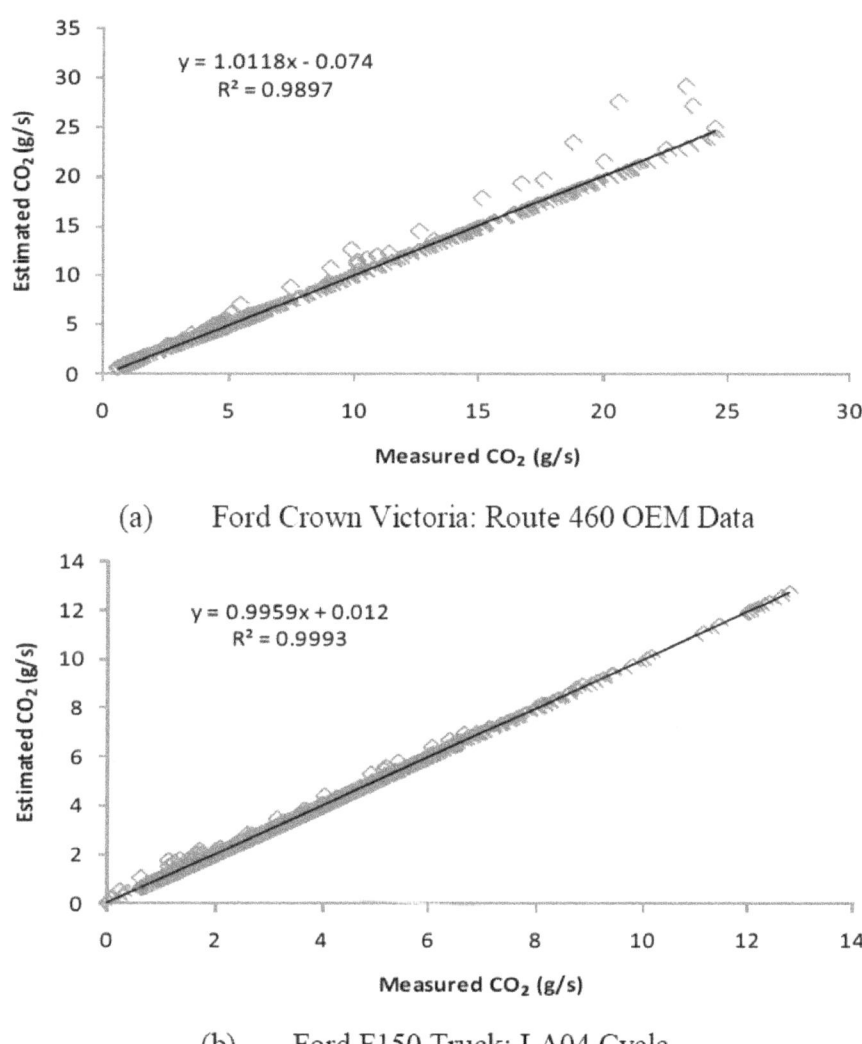

(a)   Ford Crown Victoria: Route 460 OEM Data

(b)   Ford F150 Truck: LA04 Cycle

Figure 17: CO_2 Estimation Using Fuel Consumption Rate

2.5 VT-CPFM Calibration and Validation

The VT-CPFM provides reliable estimates compared to the field-measured fuel consumption rates. However, the aforementioned validation efforts mostly rely on chassis dynamometer tests and predefined drive cycles. Given that the objective of the VT-CPFM development is to use the model as a critical component for eco-friendly systems such as a predictive ECC system, it would be beneficial to assess its performance relative to actual roadway measurements under real-world driving conditions. Furthermore, the performance evaluation is meaningful in the sense that fuel consumption rates under manual and conventional CC driving conditions may be of interest. Therefore, this section quantifies the performance of the VT-CPFM considering various vehicles on real roadway sections under either manual or conventional CC driving scenarios.

2.5.1 Collection of Field Data

Experiments were conducted on a section of Interstate 81 between mile markers 118 and 132 in order to collect fuel consumption rates under actual driving conditions. The test section was selected because it comprises various uphill and downhill sections and thus provides a suitable environment to test different engine load conditions under manual and conventional CC driving scenarios. Specifically, the northbound and the southbound directions can be considered a 1.3% downhill and a 1.3% uphill section, respectively, as the difference in altitude between the start and end points of the section is approximately 280 m across 22.4 km (14 miles). However, the roadway grade on the section varies between ± 4%. There are two 4% uphill sections that have an additional truck-climbing lane.

For the test, six light-duty vehicles, including four passenger cars and two sport utility vehicles (SUVs), were used during the experiments: a 2001 SAAB 95, a 2006 Mercedes R350, a 2008 Chevy Tahoe, a 2007 Chevy Malibu, a 2008 Chevy Malibu Hybrid, and a 2011 Toyota Camry. The six vehicles were selected to test different manufacturers, model years, and types. The Chevy Tahoe is the heaviest and most powerful vehicle while the Malibu is the lightest and least powerful car. The SAAB 95 is the oldest car and has a turbocharged engine so it generates relatively more power than the other passenger cars when considering their engine sizes.

For the collection of vehicle operation variables and fuel consumption rates an OBD II reader (the DashDaq XL device that is manufactured by Drew Technologies, Inc.) was used. The DashDaq can be easily attached to a window using a shield mount and can log and save up to 16 user-defined parameters [40]. This study selected the following 16 signals to record: absolute throttle position, fuel economy across distance, engine speed, vehicle speed, acceleration level, vehicle power, GPS-calculated speed, latitude, longitude, torque, calculated mass air flow, altitude, air flow rate from mass air flow, accelerator pedal position, fuel economy over time, and fuel level. The signals were saved to a Secure Digital (SD) card with a timestamp. The vehicle signals continued to be displayed on the screen as they were being saved to the card.

Given that the DashDaq provides the fuel economy in units of miles per gallon (MPG) along with a timestamp, instantaneous fuel consumption rates can be calculated from the recorded data. Specifically, the DashDaq calculates the fuel economy using the vehicle speed and mass air flow signals together with two assumptions. The first assumption is that the stoichiometric ratio, also called air-fuel ratio, is 14.7. The density of fuel is assumed to be 720 grams per liter. The fuel economy can then be calculated using Equation (40). Note that the first assumption is not 100% accurate given that the air-fuel ratio does not remain constant and can vary depending on the required power levels. In other words, it does not capture fuel-rich and fuel-lean conditions accurately, so the fuel estimation from this approach may slightly deviate from the true value.

$$FE = \frac{vsd}{a} \qquad\qquad (40)$$

Where FE is the fuel efficiency in MPG, v is the velocity of the vehicle in miles per hour (mph), s is the stoichiometric ratio, d is the density of fuel in grams per gallon, and a is the mass air flow in grams per hour.

The experiments were conducted during off-peak hours between 9 a.m. and 3 p.m. in order to reduce conflicts with other vehicles and secure freedom of driving. Each vehicle was driven 10 times (circulations between mile markers 118 and 132) by two different drivers: five times with the CC enabled and five times with the CC disabled. Consequently, four data sets were obtained for each vehicle: the northbound with and without CC enabled and the southbound with and without CC enabled. There was an exception with the Toyota Camry due to a roadway maintenance event. Only six circulations were completed, and the last of the experiments could not be conducted due the limited use of the roadway. The drivers participating in the study were educated about the overall procedures before the experiments. Specifically, the drivers were directed to maintain a 65 mph speed in a typical driving manner while the CC was not used (manual). However, some deviations from the target speed were allowed as needed in order to secure the driver's safety. For the CC driving experiments, the target speed was also set to 65 mph. The drivers were allowed to turn off the CC system for their safety as needed.

2.5.2 Calibration of the VT-CPFM

The specifications of the test vehicles were gathered using publicly available data sources, which included the vehicle manuals, the official sites of the vehicle manufacturers, and other car review sites [41]. Additionally, information about the vehicles was retrieved using the vehicle identification numbers (VINs) [42]. The specification information collected from different data sources was verified before calibrating the coefficients of the VT-CPFMs. For cases in which the specifications could not be obtained from the aforementioned sources, typical values were used during the calibration [20]. These included the coefficients of roadway friction and the coefficients of rolling resistance.

The specifications that were used to calibrate the VT-CPFMs are shown in Table 3 along with the data sources. Given the specifications, the VT-CPFMs for the test vehicles were calibrated using the calibration tool that was developed in the MATLAB environment. Additional details about the tool are available in the literature [39].

Table 3: Specifications of the Test Vehicles

Description	Saab 95	Mercedes R350	Tahoe	Malibu	Malibu Hybrid	Camry	Source
Trim	4dr Sedan base	Base	LS 2WD	LS	Base	LE	
Model Year	2001	2006	2008	2007	2008	2011	
Wheel Radius	0.32145	0.36865	0.4014	0.32375	0.3322	0.3322	
Redline RPM	6000	6400	7000	6000	6000	6300	
Drag Coefficient	0.29	0.31	0.39	0.34	0.34	0.28	
Frontal Area (m^2)	2.288	2.911	3.456	2.318	2.313	2.424	
Wheel Slippage	0.035	0.035	0.035	0.035	0.035	0.035	
Number of Cylinders	4	6	8	4	4	4	
Engine Size (L)	2.3	3.5	5.3	2.2	2.4	2.5	
Number of Gears	4	7	4	4	4	6	Auto website
First-gear Ratio	3.67	4.38	3.06	2.96	2.96	3.54	
Second-gear Ratio	2.1	2.86	1.63	1.62	1.62	2.05	
Third-gear Ratio	1.39	1.92	1	1	1	1.38	
Fourth-gear Ratio	1	1.37	0.7	0.68	0.68	0.98	
Fifth-gear Ratio	-	1	-	-	-	0.74	
Sixth-gear Ratio	-	0.82	-	-	-	0.66	
Seventh-gear Ratio	-	0.73	-	-	-	-	
Final Drive Ratio	2.56	3.9	3.23	3.63	3.63	3.82	
Mass (kg)	1601	2190	2388	1440	1604	1500	
City Fuel Efficiency	21	16	14	24	24	22	
Hwy Fuel Efficiency	30	21	20	34	32	33	
Rolling Coefficient (Cr)	1.75	1.75	1.75	1.75	1.75	1.75	Rakha et al., 2001
c_1	0.0328	0.0328	0.0328	0.0328	0.0328	0.0328	
c_2	4.575	4.575	4.575	4.575	4.575	4.575	
Driveline Efficiency	0.92	0.92	0.92	0.92	0.92	0.92	
P_{mfo}(Pa)	400000	400000	400000	400000	400000	400000	Wong, 2001
Q (J/kg)	43000000	43000000	43000000	43000000	43000000	43000000	
Idling Speed (rpm)	820	700	600	680	660	660	Field Data

2.6 Validation of the VT-CPFM

2.6.1 Instantaneous Fuel Consumption Rates

Given the calibrated VT-CPFM parameters, the fuel consumption estimates and measurements were compared to validate the performance of the VT-CPFM and the calibration procedure. In order to calculate the instantaneous fuel consumption rates, the power levels were first computed given that they are required as inputs to the model. Roadway grade, which is used to compute the grade-resistance force, was initially calculated using the x, y coordinates and height signals collected by the GPS unit. However, the resolution of the GPS height signal was found to not be sufficiently accurate for computational purposes. Thus, higher resolution geographical data were obtained from NAVTEQ and were used to compute the grade-resistance force.

Given the field-measured fuel consumption rates and model estimates, the quality of the fuel estimates were first assessed using scatter plots. Specifically, the field-measured fuel consumption rates were plotted along the x-axis, and the model estimates were plotted along the y-axis. A regression line was then fitted to the scattered data points so that one can visually determine that the estimates are close to the field measurements, as illustrated in Figure 18. Note that the regression line was forced to intersect with the origin (0, 0) when fitting to the data. The slope of the line indicates whether the VT-CPFM overestimates or underestimates the field measurements. The coefficient of determination indicates the degree of error that the model produces. For example, the slope of the regression line in Figure 18 is 0.93, which means that the model underestimates the fuel consumption levels by 7 percent (on average). The R^2 value of the regression line is 0.9817, which is very close to 1. This implies that the model has a marginal error of less than 2 percent.

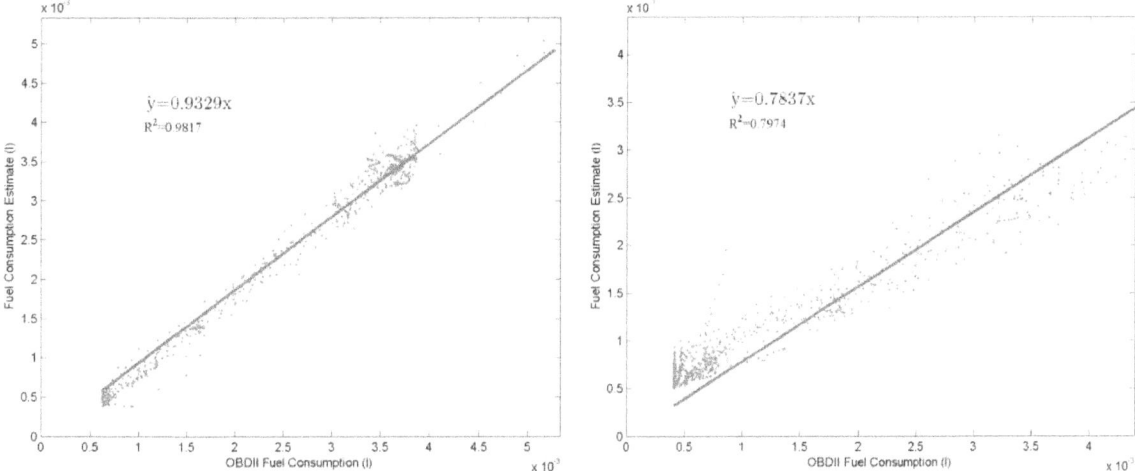

Figure 18: Fuel Measurements versus Fuel Estimates Scatter Plots with a Regression Line

The instantaneous estimated and measured fuel consumption levels for each of the trips (i.e., the speed profiles along the study section) are compared and summarized in Table 4. The slope and R^2 values were averaged by vehicle type (six vehicles), driving direction (southbound and northbound), and driving type (manual driving and CC driving). The results demonstrate that the performance of the VT-CPFM mainly depend on the vehicle type regardless of the driving direction and driving type. It is demonstrated that the fuel consumption rates estimated by the VT-CPFM-1 models were generally greater than those estimated by the VT-CPFM-2 models.

The VT-CPFM model estimates for the SAAB 95 and the Mercedes R350 appeared to be overestimated. However, their R^2 values were still very close to 1, demonstrating that the models provided ideal estimates that follow the same trends as observed from the OBD reading estimates. Figure 19 shows that the fuel estimates follow the same peaks and valleys observed during the field measurements, although the fuel consumption rates estimated by the R350 model are higher than the fuel measurements. Overall, the VT-CPFMs were shown to provide ideal estimates given that the R^2 values were very close to 1. All R^2 values were greater than 0.85. Specifically, the profile shown in Figure 19(b) is one that has the lowest R^2 values, but it still shows a good match to the field measurements.

Table 4: Average Slope and R^2 Values for the Regression Lines

Classification			VT-CPFM-1		VT-CPFM-2	
			Slope	R^2	Slope	R^2
95	Southbound	Manual	1.40	0.95	1.18	0.96
		Cruise	1.43	0.96	1.19	0.97
	Northbound	Manual	1.37	0.95	1.19	0.97
		Cruise	1.42	0.96	1.22	0.98
R350	Southbound	Manual	1.61	0.95	1.46	0.96
		Cruise	1.62	0.96	1.46	0.96
	Northbound	Manual	1.56	0.93	1.42	0.95
		Cruise	1.62	0.96	1.48	0.97
Tahoe	Southbound	Manual	1.04	0.95	0.92	0.95
		Cruise	1.02	0.94	0.90	0.94
	Northbound	Manual	1.11	0.95	0.99	0.95
		Cruise	1.13	0.94	1.00	0.93
Malibu	Southbound	Manual	1.26	0.95	1.01	0.95
		Cruise	1.32	0.97	1.04	0.97
	Northbound	Manual	1.29	0.96	1.04	0.98
		Cruise	1.29	0.97	1.04	0.97
Malibu Hybrid	Southbound	Manual	0.97	0.94	0.82	0.95
		Cruise	0.93	0.98	0.79	0.97
	Northbound	Manual	0.97	0.96	0.85	0.98
		Cruise	0.94	0.97	0.82	0.98
Camry	Southbound	Manual	0.94	0.92	0.72	0.91
		Cruise	0.96	0.90	0.74	0.90
	Northbound	Manual	0.98	0.90	0.76	0.83
		Cruise	1.02	0.87	0.79	0.80

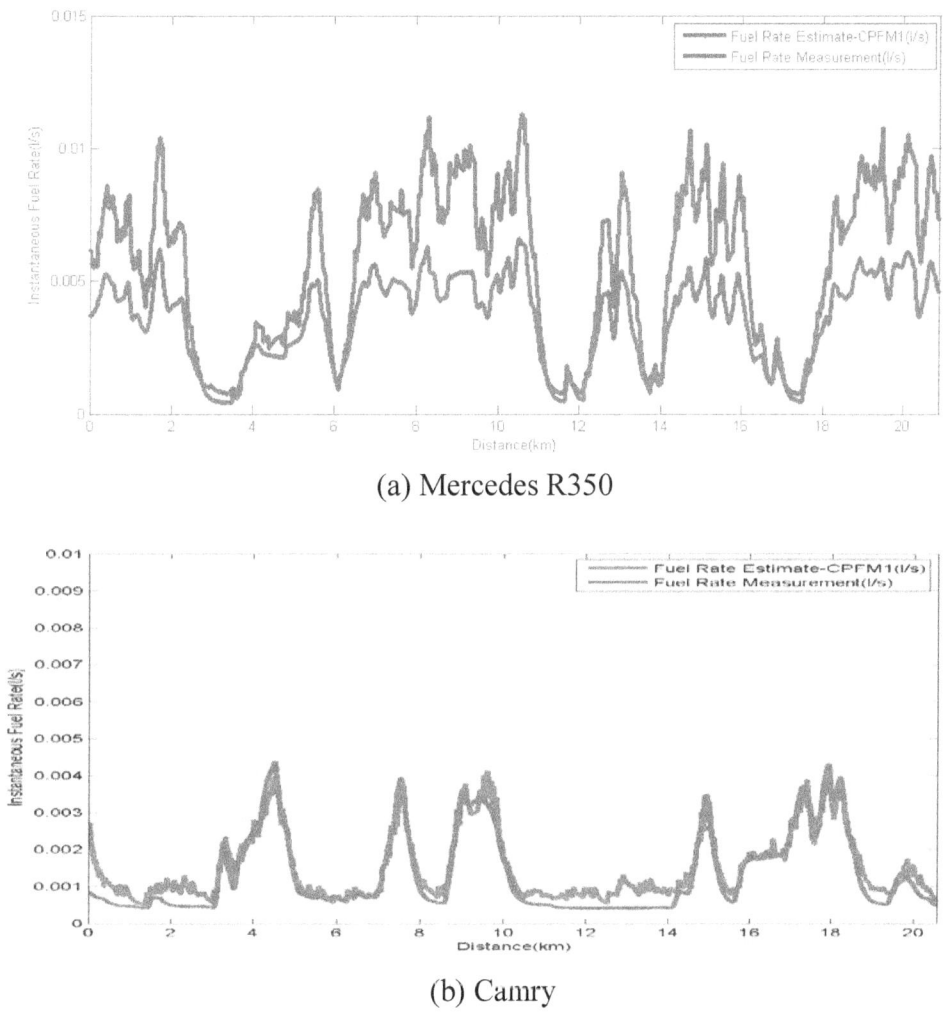

(a) Mercedes R350

(b) Camry

Figure 19: Fuel Consumption Profile on a Test Run

2.6.2 Comparison of Fuel Economy

The fuel economy values estimated using the VT-CPFM models were compared to the field-measured values in order to quantify how consistent the aggregated estimates were when compared with the field data. The average fuel economy values and relative differences are summarized in Table 5. Given that some of the models overestimated the fuel consumption levels, the fuel economy estimated by the models was lower than the field measurements. Specifically, the differences in fuel efficiency estimates between the VT-CPFM-1 model and OBD estimates ranged from 36 to 11 percent, while those of the VT-CPFM-2 model ranged from 30 to 36 percent. Consequently, it appears that the VT-CPFM-2 model produced greater differences as compared to the field measurements.

Table 5: Fuel Economy and Relative Difference

Classification			Fuel Efficiency (km/l)			Relative Difference	
			OBD-II	CPFM-1	CPFM-2	CPFM-1	CPFM-2
95	SB	Manual	10.9	8.0	9.3	-27%	-14%
		Cruise	11.4	8.1	9.6	-29%	-16%
	NB	Manual	17.9	14.0	15.1	-22%	-16%
		Cruise	19.9	15.2	16.2	-24%	-19%
R350	SB	Manual	8.2	5.2	5.8	-36%	-30%
		Cruise	8.4	5.3	5.9	-36%	-30%
	NB	Manual	14.0	10.0	10.6	-29%	-24%
		Cruise	15.3	10.3	11.0	-33%	-28%
Tahoe	SB	Manual	7.5	7.2	8.1	-3%	9%
		Cruise	7.4	7.3	8.3	-1%	11%
	NB	Manual	14.0	11.9	13.4	-15%	-4%
		Cruise	14.6	12.1	13.5	-17%	-7%
Malibu	SB	Manual	11.8	9.4	11.7	-20%	0%
		Cruise	12.3	9.5	11.9	-23%	-4%
	NB	Manual	19.9	16.2	19.1	-19%	-4%
		Cruise	20.0	16.0	19.0	-20%	-5%
Malibu Hybrid	SB	Manual	11.0	11.6	13.5	5%	22%
		Cruise	10.9	11.9	13.7	9%	26%
	NB	Manual	17.8	19.2	20.8	8%	17%
		Cruise	18.9	21.1	22.4	11%	18%
Camry	SB	Manual	11.9	12.4	16.2	5%	36%
		Cruise	12.0	12.2	15.8	2%	31%
	NB	Manual	21.1	19.9	24.7	-6%	17%
		Cruise	21.5	19.3	24.1	-10%	12%

Given that the fuel consumption models are used for comparison of alternative scenarios, the fuel economy estimates are compared in terms of relative differences. In other words, it is important to evaluate the effectiveness of the models in identifying the optimum scenario. For this analysis, the manual driving and CC driving scenarios were compared with regard to fuel economy. Additionally, driving on Interstate 81 Northbound and Southbound was tested. The fuel economy values that were averaged across all vehicles by the driving direction and the driving type are summarized in Table 6. The field data indicate that the fuel economy was 4.1 percent greater when the CC system was engaged, demonstrating that the conventional CC driving is better than manual driving in terms of fuel economy. The VT-CPFM-1 and -2 model estimates also demonstrate that the CC driving is better than manual driving with regard to fuel economy (2.3 and 1.8 percent improvement, respectively).

The field data showed that the fuel economy of driving along the northbound test section of Interstate 81 was 73.8 percent greater than driving in the southbound direction. The VT-CPFM-1 and -2 model estimates also resulted in consistent outcomes given that the fuel economy values for driving along the northbound direction were estimated to be 71.1 and 61.9 percent greater, respectively, as illustrated in Figure 20.

Table 6: Fuel Economy Averaged across All Vehicles

Classification		Fuel Efficiency (km/l)		
		OBD-II	CPFM-1	CPFM-2
SB	Manual	10.21	8.98	10.76
	Cruise	10.41	9.06	10.84
NB	Manual	17.46	15.20	17.28
	Cruise	18.38	15.67	17.71

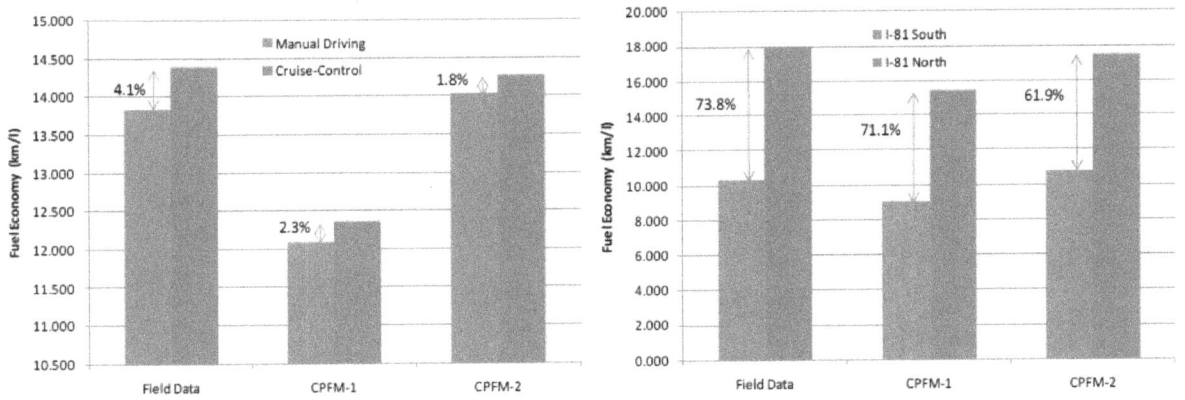

Figure 20: Comparison of Field Data with the VT-CPFM Estimates

2.6.3 Comparison to Coefficients Calibrated using Field Data

Since the VT-CPFMs, which are calibrated using the EPA ratings (referred to as EPA models hereafter), tended to overestimate fuel consumption levels, the calibration of the models was conducted using the second-by-second OBD-gathered data (referred to as Field models hereafter) in order to ascertain the reason for these differences. Thus, the VT-CPFMs were first fitted to the field measurements as shown in Figure 21. Specifically, the field-measured fuel consumption rates were plotted versus the vehicle power estimates. A second-order polynomial was then fitted to the data. As seen in the figure, the EPA models for the Saab 95, the Mercedes R350, and the Malibu appear to be inconsistent with the field measurements while the Field models fit well to the measurements.

The differences in the fuel estimation are demonstrated in Figure 22, which features scatter plots and fuel consumption rates across the distance traveled. The scatter plots show the fuel consumption rates estimated by each of the EPA and Field models for the Mercedes R350 across the fuel consumption measurements. As can be seen in the figure, the Field model shows a significant improvement in the fuel estimation when compared to the EPA model. The subplots (c) and (d) also demonstrate that the fuel consumption estimated using the Field model is consistent with the field measurements.

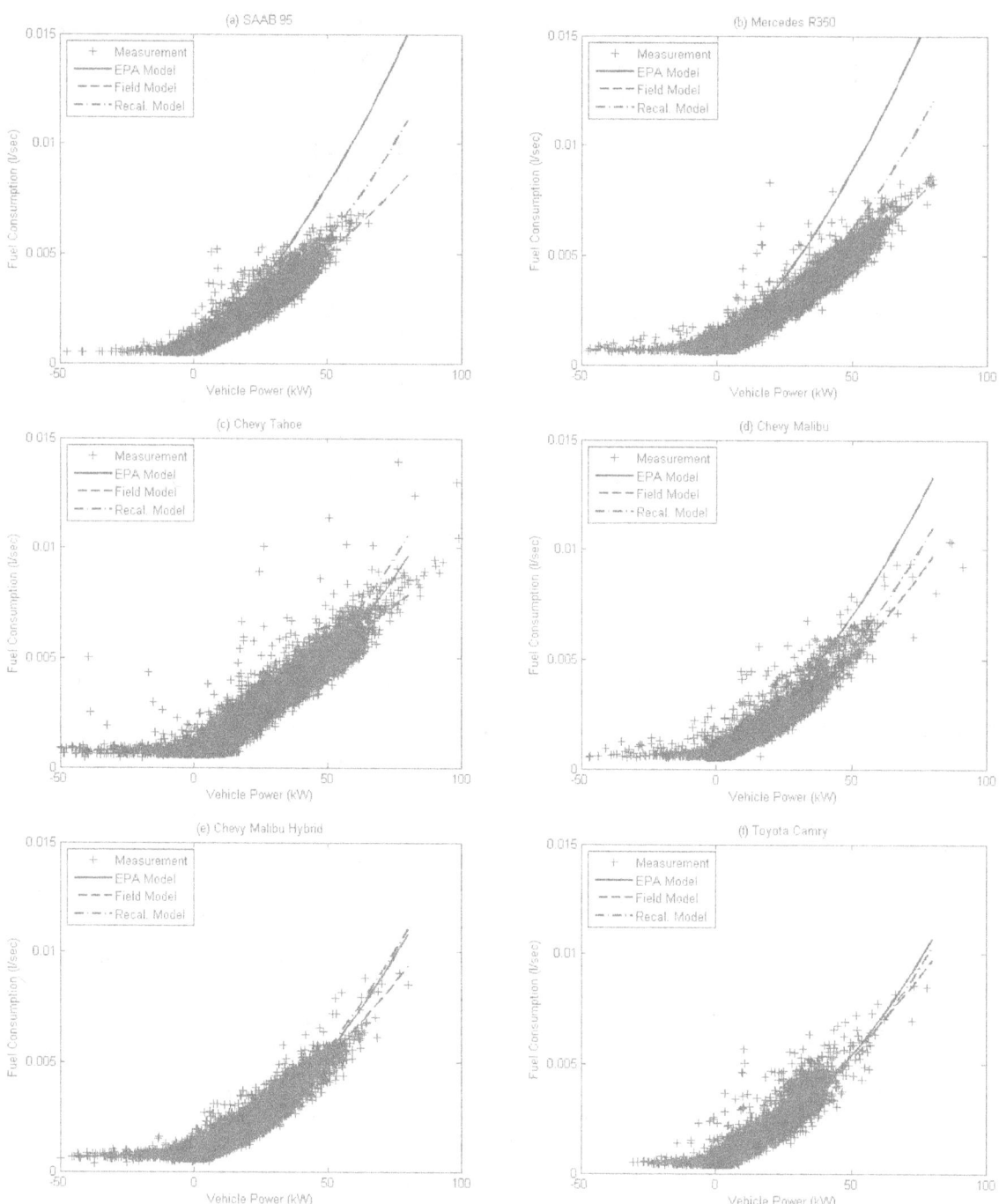

Figure 21: EPA, Field, and Recalibrated Models

Figure 22: Comparison of Fuel Consumption Estimates on a Test Run (Mercedes R350)

Given that the Field models fit well to the field measurements, the city and highway fuel economy ratings estimated using the Field models were recomputed. The results demonstrate significant differences in the fuel economy ratings for some cases, as demonstrated in Table 7. For example, the highway fuel economy of the Mercedes R350 is rated at 21.0 MPG by the EPA, but it is estimated at 29.6 MPG by running the Field model on the EPA drive cycles. These results reveal that the fuel economy ratings by the EPA are not consistent with what was observed in the field for some vehicles. These differences can either be attributed to errors in the computation of the fuel rates based on the fuel-to-air ratio, or could be attributed to errors in the EPA ratings, or errors in both. In this analysis, the OBD fuel estimates were assumed to be correct and the EPA ratings were adjusted to match the field measurements.

Table 7: Comparison of Fuel Economy Ratings

Vehicle	Fuel Economy Rated by EPA (MPG)		Fuel Economy Estimated by Field Model (MPG)		Relative Difference	
	City	Highway	City	Highway	City	Highway
Saab 95	21.0	30.0	23.3	38.9	11%	30%
Mercedes R350	16.0	21.0	18.7	29.6	17%	41%
Tahoe	17.3	27.7	23.7	28.1	37%	1%
Malibu	24.0	34.0	26.1	42.7	9%	26%
Malibu Hybrid	30.7	45.1	24.6	39.7	-20%	-12%
Camry	28.0	46.6	28.5	44.2	2%	-5%

In order to ascertain that the VT-CPFM framework is valid, the VT-CPFMs (referred to as Recalibrated models hereafter) were calibrated using the fuel economy ratings estimated based on the field measurements using Equations (4) through (7) then compared to the instantaneous field measurements. Once both sets of the models were consistent with each other with regard to the fuel consumption estimation, it was concluded that the structure of the VT-CPFM is valid. As can be seen in Figure 21, the Recalibrated models fit well to the field measurements, as do the Field models. Additionally, the slopes and R^2 values of the regression lines are fitted to the scatter plots of the fuel estimates computed by the Recalibrated models and the field measurements are as close to 1 as those of the Field models. The average slopes and R^2 values are summarized in Table 8 by test vehicle and model. As seen in Table 8, the Recalibrated models show a significant improvement in the fuel consumption estimation when compared to the EPA models. In other words, it can be concluded that the structure of the VT-CPFM provides a practical, valid method to estimate fuel consumption rates. However, the fuel economy ratings quantified by the EPA show discrepancies when compared to those estimated by the Field models.

Table 8: Summary of Average Slopes and R^2 Values

Vehicle	EPA Model		Field Model		Recalibrated Model	
	Slope	R^2	Slope	R^2	Slope	R^2
Saab 95	1.41	0.95	0.97	0.97	0.97	0.97
Mercedes R350	1.60	0.95	0.98	0.98	1.10	0.96
Tahoe	1.07	0.95	1.05	0.96	1.12	0.96
Malibu	1.29	0.96	1.00	0.97	0.99	0.97
Malibu Hybrid	0.95	0.96	1.00	0.97	1.00	0.97
Toyota Camry	0.97	0.90	1.02	0.90	0.93	0.84

2.7 Conclusions

The study develops two simple fuel consumption models that do not result in a bang-bang control system and that can be calibrated easily using publicly available data. Specifically, the models can be calibrated using the EPA city and highway fuel economy ratings that are publicly available. The models are demonstrated to estimate vehicle fuel consumption rates consistent with in-field measurements (coefficient of determination above 0.90). Also, a procedure for estimating CO_2 emissions is developed, producing emission estimates that are highly correlated with field measurements (greater than 0.98). This study also validates the VT-CPFMs by comparing the field-measured fuel consumption rates with the model estimates. From the comparison results, the VT-CPFMs calibrated using the city and highway fuel economy values are proven to generally provide reliable fuel consumption estimates. More importantly, both estimates and measurements have the same behavioral changes depending on engine load conditions. The study shows that the values of the coefficient of determination are close to 1, demonstrating the consistency of the VT-CPFM. The proposed model can be integrated within a traffic simulation framework to quantify the energy and environmental impacts of traffic operational projects. Furthermore, the proposed models can be used to develop a predictive ECC system.

3. COMPARISON OF MANUAL DRIVING AND CONVENTIONAL CRUISE CONTROL

This section quantifies the fuel efficiency impacts of using a CC system relative to manual driving based on field driving tests. CC (or autocruise) is a device or system that is frequently used while driving, especially on highways, as it automatically controls the speed of a vehicle as set by the driver. Consequently, using CC reduces the driver's fatigue and improves comfort. As fuel prices change significantly, the fuel savings that result from the use of CC have recently attracted attention. From a fuel-saving perspective, CC use is recommended as one of the eco-driving tips by many organizations .

CC was invented in 1945 by Ralph Teetor, and the system was initially installed into the Chrysler Imperial in 1958 [24]. Automotive electronic CC, which is the electrical version of CC that uses digital memory, was invented by Daniel Aaron Wisner in 1968. An extensive adaptation of CC was achieved following development by Motorola, Inc. of an integrated circuit. Most cars currently manufactured in the United States are fitted with a CC system that uses a specific control algorithm that depends on the manufacturers.

As mentioned earlier, it is widely known that the use of CC on highways can save gas. However, it is difficult to find literature that proves CC's effectiveness in a quantitative manner with regard to fuel savings even though this idea seems to be accepted by the public. One study conducted by Edmunds.com concluded that an average fuel economy savings of 7 percent resulted from the use of CC [45]. However, it is not clear how the effectiveness will vary if the system is used on uphill or downhill sections. It is recommended that CC be disabled on hilly terrain because the system tries to maintain even speeds on steep hills, thus resulting in high fuel consumption [41]. The literature indicates that experienced drivers can manually drive in a more fuel-efficient manner than by enabling CC driving [46]. Consequently, there is a need to test the effectiveness of using CC in a systematic way based on field driving tests. Specifically, the objectives of this study are to test: 1) if conventional CC driving can significantly save fuel compared to manual driving, and 2) whether fuel savings remain constant when driving on uphill and downhill sections of a roadway. The study utilized the data collected on a section of I-81, which was described earlier.

3.1 Manual Driving and Cruise Control Driving Test Results

3.1.1 Speed and Throttle Control

The field test results show that the CC systems demonstrated a good ability to maintain a constant speed. Overall, the systems maintained the vehicle speed close to the target speed of 65 mph during most of the test runs. As shown in Figure 23 (which includes some sample speed profiles from the test runs), the speeds of the individual vehicles were maintained close to the target speed with marginal errors. However, it is interesting to note that the control logics of the systems are distinct from each other. Figure 23(c) clearly shows that the Chevy Tahoe, which is the heaviest car amongst the test vehicles, accelerated on the downhill sections and returned to the target speed after passing the downhill sections. Additionally, the Toyota Camry CC system also seems to have similar control logic to the Tahoe although the speed does not increase as much as that of the Tahoe. The speed profiles of the Tahoe and the Toyota Camry are different from the speed profiles of the other systems while driving on the downhill sections. The systems of the Tahoe and the Toyota Camry seem to allow the vehicle to utilize their gravitational force, which might affect fuel economy rather than braking to maintain the target speed.

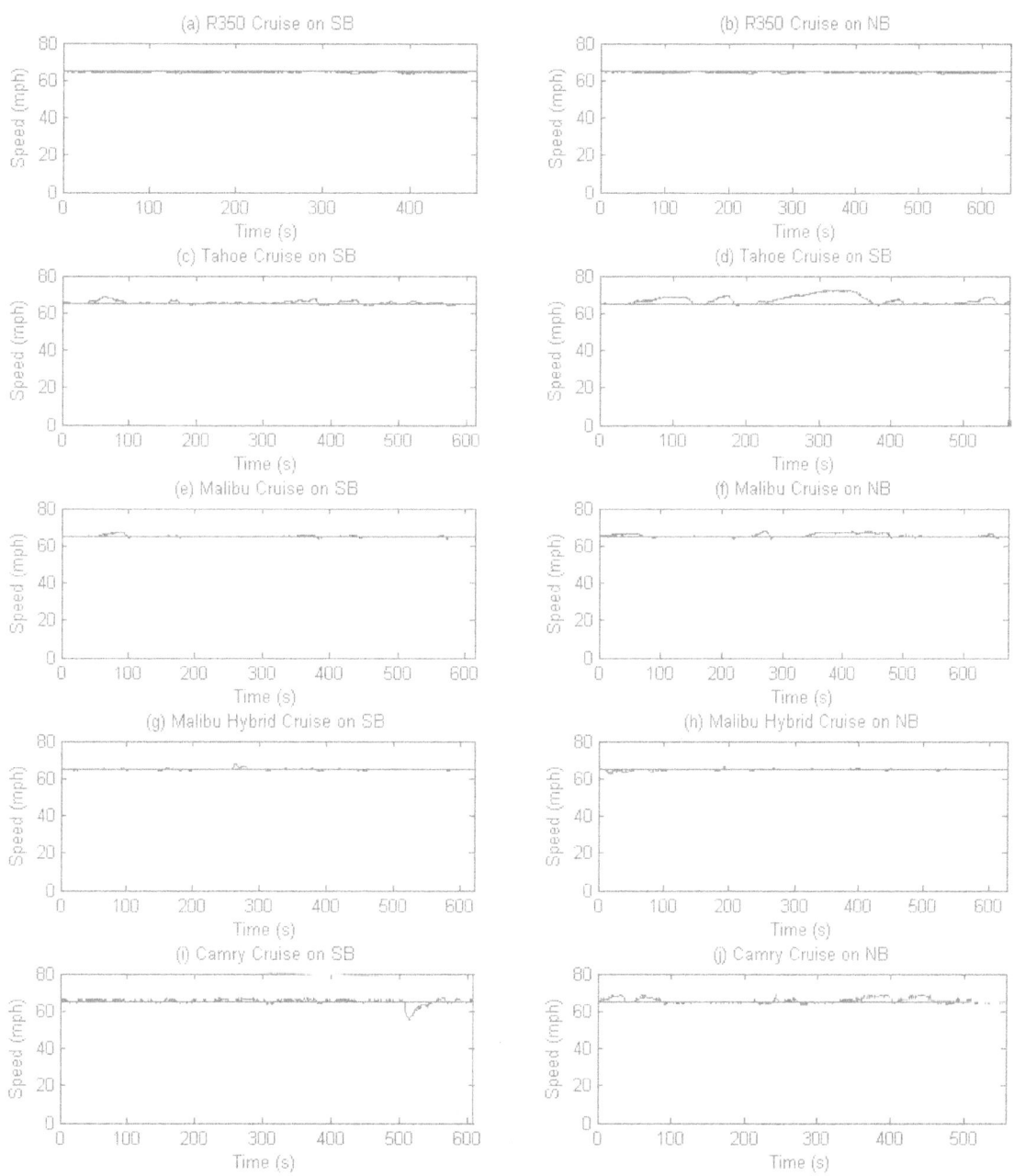

Figure 23: Speed Profiles under Cruise Control System

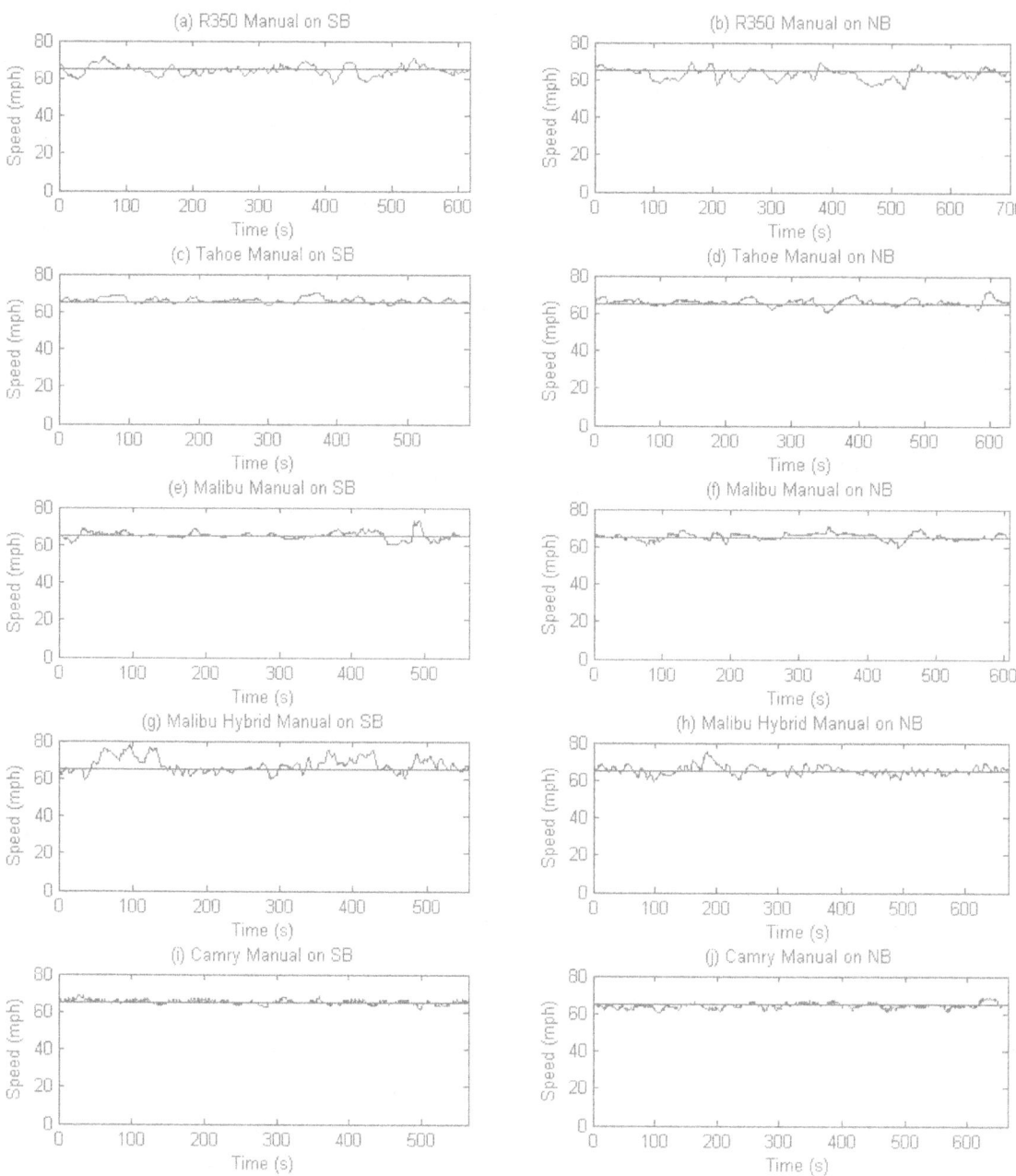

Figure 24: Speed Profiles under Manual Driving

Conversely, the drivers of the test vehicles were capable of manually maintaining the target speed. However, it was observed that manual driving cannot generally control the speed as precisely as a CC system. This can be clearly confirmed in Figure 24. The deviations of the manual driving test runs from the target speed appeared greater than those of the CC driving test runs. This fact can be reconfirmed since the standard deviations of the speed measurements of the manual driving test runs were greater than those of CC driving. However, it is demonstrated that some of the drivers manually achieved more precise control of the target speed than when using the CC system. For example, based on the test results of the Toyota Camry, the standard deviation of the CC driving tests on the southbound lanes was greater than that of the manual driving tests, as can be seen in Table 9.

Table 9: Average Speed (Km/H) And Standard Deviation of the Speed Measurements

Classification		Southbound		Northbound	
		Manual	Cruise	Manual	Cruise
R350	Avg. Speed	102.8	102.8	102.8	101.9
	Std. Dev.	4.2	0.6	3.9	2.9
TAHOE	Avg. Speed	104.7	104.9	105.3	106.7
	Std. Dev.	2.7	2.0	3.4	4.5
MALIBU	Avg. Speed	102.7	104.9	104.7	104.7
	Std. Dev.	4.0	2.3	3.0	3.5
MALIBU HYBRID	Avg. Speed	103.9	103.9	103.9	104.1
	Std. Dev.	5.6	2.3	5.1	2.8
TOYOTA CAMRY	Avg. Speed	103.7	103.0	103.3	105.4
	Std. Dev.	2.7	3.5	3.0	3.0

With regard to throttle control, one would expect that the CC throttle control would be more stable than manual control (i.e., without significant abrupt changes in throttling) when compared to manual driving. Figure 25(a) clearly demonstrates that Driver-1 frequently alternated between pressing the accelerator pedal and the brake pedal, especially when driving on the uphill and downhill sections. Consequently, it can be concluded that Driver-1 is not a skilled driver at controlling the vehicle throttle. Interestingly, the throttle control profiles of the Driver-1 manual and CC driving tests were similar to each other in the sense that the general patterns of throttle positions were identically sensitive to the gradients of the roadway. However, they are clearly distinct because the manual driving test had greater throttle positions. This is one of the critical reasons why using the CC systems generally saved gas. In terms of fuel economy, it was observed that the fuel economy values of the CC and manual driving tests plotted in Figure 25(a) were 21.3 MPG and 20.4 MPG, respectively. Thus, using CC for Driver-1 resulted in a 3-percent increase in vehicle mileage when compared to manual driving. Figure 25(b) is a profile of a different driver (Driver-2) who experienced the identical experimental setting as Driver-1. As can be seen, the Driver-2 throttle control was better than that of Driver-1 since the peaks in the throttle positions were generally lower than those of Driver-1.

There was another interesting result found with regard to throttle control. There may be several factors contributing to the throttle position controlled by the CC systems, such as vehicle specification, driving environment, CC logic, etc. However, it can be confirmed that the throttle control logic is one of the most critical factors that results in differences in the throttle positions. As can be seen in Figure 26, the Toyota Camry and Chevy Malibu ideally maintained the target speed of 65 mph during a test run, but the throttle position profiles of the two vehicles were clearly distinct from each other.

Figure 25: Throttle Profiles

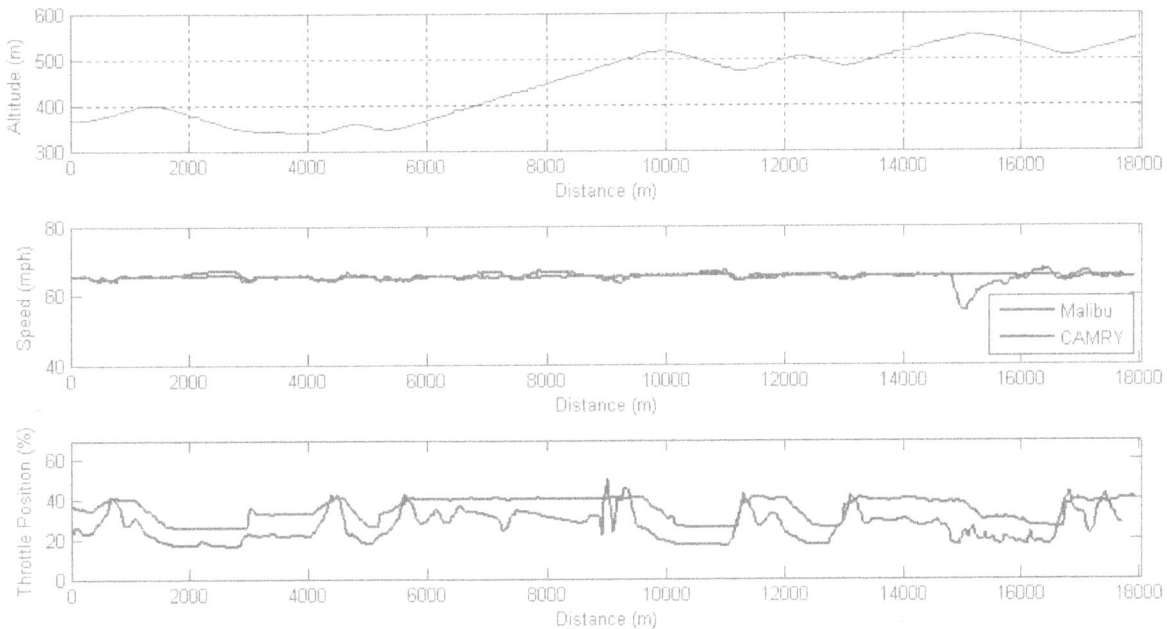

Figure 26: Cruise Control Profiles of Malibu and Camry

3.1.2 Fuel Economy

The test results clearly demonstrated that using the CC systems resulted in a fuel economy enhancement. As can be seen in Table 10, the fuel economy values of the CC driving tests were greater than those of the manual driving tests, although there were some variations in the differences depending on the driver, the vehicle, and the direction of travel. The average fuel economy enhancement across all the field tests was 3.3 percent. It is interesting to note that using CC on the northbound section, which is mostly downhill as a whole, resulted in better fuel economy than using it on the southbound section. Another interesting finding was that the fuel economy enhancement ranged from 0.2% to 10.5%, demonstrating that changes in driving behavior significantly affect the vehicle fuel economy.

Table 10: Fuel Economy of Manual Driving and CC Driving

Classification	Southbound			Northbound		
	Manual (MPG)	Cruise (MPG)	Relative Diff.	Manual (MPG)	Cruise (MPG)	Relative Diff.
R350	20.4	21.0	3.0%	32.0	35.3	10.5%
TAHOE	18.8	18.8	0.2%	32.2	33.6	4.5%
MALIBU	29.6	30.8	3.8%	46.0	46.7	1.7%
MALIBU HYBRID	27.5	27.7	0.7%	41.0	43.5	6.0%
CAMRY	30.1	30.5	1.5%	48.4	49.7	2.8%
Average	25.3	25.8	1.9%	39.9	41.8	4.7%

Based on the test results, manual driving and CC driving were not significantly different from each other with regard to travel time, as can be seen in Table 11. The relative differences ranged from -2.0% to 1.4%. Consequently, it can be concluded that using conventional CC devices can save a significant amount of fuel without a significant loss of travel time.

Table 11: Travel Times of Manual Driving and CC Driving

Classification	Southbound			Northbound		
	Manual	Cruise	Relative Diff.	Manual	Cruise	Relative Diff.
R350	616	616	0.0%	680	678	-0.3%
TAHOE	605	613	1.4%	657	647	-1.4%
MALIBU	611	604	-1.1%	660	658	-0.4%
MALIBU HYBRID	610	615	0.8%	665	664	-0.1%
CAMRY	611	615	0.7%	669	656	-2.0%
Average	611	613	0.4%	666	661	-0.8%

As illustrated in Figure 25, some differences were found in the throttle control levels between the various drivers. Figure 25 demonstrates that Driver-2 drove more efficiently with regard to fuel savings when compared to Driver-1. In order to assess the differences between the drivers, a comparison of fuel consumption by the different drivers was conducted, and a summary of the results is presented in Table 12. Specifically, the fuel consumption values in Table 12 were computed by averaging all test runs by the individual drivers; in some cases, the values were averaged across more than one test vehicle. As is clearly seen, the average difference between the CC and manual driving tests of Driver-1 was greater than that of Driver-2. Driver-3 was the most skilled driver amongst the subjects as the manual driving of Driver-3 resulted in less fuel consumption than the CC driving. This confirms the fact that skilled driving can save more fuel than using CC, which is addressed in the literature [46].

Table 12: Fuel Consumptions (L) by Test Vehicle Drivers

Driver Index	Northbound			Southbound		
	Cruise	Manual	Diff (%)	Cruise	Manual	Diff (%)
1	1 35	1.48	9%	1.98	2.07	5%
2	1 29	1.37	7%	2 01	2.08	3%
3	1 22	1.19	-2%	1 83	1.8	-1%
4	1 35	1.43	6%	2 28	2.18	-4%
5	0.94	0.97	3%	1 36	1.38	2%
6	1 07	1.15	8%	1 53	1.53	0%
7	1 07	1.12	4%	1 58	1.54	-3%

3.2 Statistical Test Results - CC Driving versus Manual Control Driving

The field-measured data demonstrate that CC driving is significantly effective with regard to fuel savings when compared to manual driving. A set of t-tests were then conducted at a 5-percent significance level (alpha = 0.05) to test if CC driving was statistically different from manual driving. Since fuel economy is sensitive to vehicle specifications and roadway conditions, the field test results (fuel consumption in liters) were classified by vehicle and roadway section and used during the t-tests. Based on the t-test results, it was demonstrated that CC driving is not, statistically, 100% different from manual driving, as can be seen in Table 13. For the R350, the difference between CC driving and manual driving was significantly different on the southbound and northbound sections because the confidence interval of the difference in the fuel use did not include zero. As it was previously found that CC driving saved more fuel on the northbound section, the differences between CC driving and manual driving were more evident on the northbound section. Overall, CC driving can be thought to be effective with regard to fuel savings, although the differences between CC driving and manual driving are not statistically significant for all test vehicles. If more test runs are conducted, the differences may be more significant.

Table 13: T-Test Results

Classification	Southbound			Northbound		
	P-value	Confidence Interval (L)		P-value	Confidence Interval (L)	
		Lower Bound	Upper Bound		Lower Bound	Upper Bound
R350	0 00	0.03	0.11	0.01	0.05	0.21
Tahoe	0 68	-0.21	0.15	0.02	0.01	0.10
Malibu	0 09	-0.01	0.11	0.97	-0.10	0.09
Malibu Hybrid	0 65	-0.09	0.06	0.04	0.01	0.12
Camry	0 31	-0.04	0.09	0.25	-0.03	0.07

Additionally, a multiple linear regression model was fitted to the measured fuel in order to gain insight into the relationship between the fuel use and other contributing factors. The framework of the regression model is formulated in Equation (41).

$$y = \beta_0 + \beta_1 A + \beta_2 B + \beta_3 C + \beta_4 D \tag{41}$$

Where βs are the coefficients, A is the driving classification (CC or manual driving), B is the vehicle classification, C is the roadway section classification (the southbound or the northbound section), and D is the driver classification.

Given that the dependent variables are non-numerical and qualitative variables, one of the categories of the dependent variables is used as the reference level. For example, Toyota Camry is used as the reference level of the B classification because "c" comes first in the alphabet. Given that the regression model has a multiple R-squared of 0.9349 and the p-value is less than 2.2e-16, the model is demonstrated to be significant and provides reliable estimates. The regression model demonstrates that manual driving consumes an average of 0.03 L more on the study sections than does CC driving, as can be seen in Table 14. However, this difference is not significant at the 5% significance level because the p-value of the β_1 coefficient of the manual driving is 0.16. For the vehicles, the R350, the Tahoe, and the Malibu Hybrid are significantly different from Toyota Camry with regard to fuel consumption on the study sections. Driving on the southbound section consumed 0.57 L more than driving on the northbound section.

Table 14: Coefficients of the Regression Model and Significances of the Coefficients

Classification		Estimate	Std. Error	t-value	p-value
β_0	Intercept	0.838807	0.038179	21.971	< 2e-16
β_1	CC	-	-	-	-
	Manual	0.033761	0.023924	1.411	0.16208
β_2	R350	0.542127	0.04927	11.003	< 2e-16
	Tahoe	0.679716	0.05998	11.332	< 2e-16
	Malibu	0.036807	0.043883	0.839	0.404102
	Malibu Hybrid	0.186299	0.049265	3.782	0 000299
	Camry	-	-	-	-
β_3	Southbound	0.569075	0.023284	24.44	< 2e-16
	Northbound	-	-	-	-
β_4	Driver-1	0.057996	0.050551	1.147	0 254689
	Driver-2	-	-	-	-
	Driver-3	0.049436	0.043087	1.147	0 254661
	Driver-4	-0 01282	0.065927	-0.194	0 846355
	Driver-5	-	-	-	-
	Driver-6	-0 00605	0.049867	-0.121	0.903774
	Driver-7	-	-	-	-

3.3 Summary of Findings

This section investigated the fuel efficiency of a CC system compared with manual driving using field data along Interstate 81. The test section was selected given that it comprises various uphill and downhill sections. The study found that the CC driving improves vehicle fuel efficiency compared to the manual driving although there were some variations in the differences depending on the driver, the vehicle, and the direction of travel. The average fuel economy enhancement across all the field tests was 3.3%. It is interesting to note that using CC on the northbound section, which includes multiple downhill sections, resulted in better fuel economy than using it on the uphill sections. Also, the study found that manual driving and CC driving were not significantly different from each other with regard to travel time. Based on the multiple linear regression model used, it was demonstrated that manual driving consumes 0.03 L more fuel on the study sections than does CC driving; however, this difference was not found to be statistically significant at a 95-percent significance level.

4. PREDICTIVE ECO-CRUISE CONTROL SYSTEM: MODEL LOGIC AND PRELIMINARY TESTING

Fuel saving is a concern for both individual drivers and the nation as a whole since fuel prices continue to change in an unpredictable manner, which affects the nation's economy as well as that of its citizens. People seem to be especially sensitive to vehicle fuel consumption because pump prices are posted everywhere. People frequently seek solutions to enhance their fuel economy by changing the factors that affect fuel consumption. One of the attractive solutions is to avoid aggressive driving behavior; this is termed eco-driving. According to Ecodrive.org, eco-driving leads to significant fuel savings. For example, an average fuel economy improvement of 24% was observed from the tests conducted by Ford [47]. Given that the surface transportation sector consumes more than 20 million barrels of fuel in the United States on a daily basis, it is expected that the fuel savings would be significant [48].

With regard to road network characteristics, roadway grade is among the biggest contributors to high fuel consumption levels because driving on a steep upgrade section requires additional power to overcome the grade resistance. Specifically, a study showed that fuel consumption rates increase by up to 18 percent on a roadway grade of 1 percent and up to 94 percent on a grade of 6 percent when compared to a level roadway [5]. Given that the impact of roadway grade on fuel consumption levels is significant, it is expected that eco-driving on hilly roadways would produce significant savings in fuel consumption. The basic driving strategy can be described as minimizing the power levels required while maintaining the vehicle speed within an acceptable speed range and transit time. Specifically, if the current roadway grade is uphill, the vehicle should be controlled to use as little power as possible to maintain the minimum level required (in other words, the minimum throttle level or pedal level). If the roadway grade is downhill, the vehicle should be controlled in order to use the force of gravity without braking.

As such, eco-driving on a hilly roadway would largely depend on the topographic information and vehicle controls. In the present day it is very common to use GPS-based navigation systems to receive driving-assistant information; consequently, topographic information can be easily assembled. However, there has been a need to develop eco-vehicle control systems. Currently, CC is a widely used system that automatically regulates the speed of a vehicle. It is a closed-loop system that controls the throttle of the car to maintain a steady speed as set by the driver. Although it clearly provides a convenience to the driver, using CC on hilly roadways is not recommended from the fuel-saving standpoint because it results in excessive fuel consumption levels in attempting to maintain the steady speed. Consequently, there exists a need to develop a CC system that reduces fuel consumption while maintaining the vehicle speed within a range as set by the driver.

The objective of this study was to develop a predictive ECC system that generates vehicle control plans for fuel-consumption reduction by utilizing topographic information. The generated plans are expressed as a sequence of vehicle speed, throttle level, braking level, and gear selection over a certain distance or time period. Specifically, the system is a predictive control system that optimizes the vehicle controls in advance while satisfying the user-specified requirements. The study utilized the VT-CPFM-1 model and the powertrain model to develop a predictive ECC system.

4.1 Development of Predictive Eco-cruise Control System

4.1.1 Framework

The objective of this predictive ECC system is to generate an optimal vehicle control plan which will result in minimized fuel use for a given road topography in a predictive manner. Hellstrom developed a predictive CC system for heavy trucks [49]. This study employs the operational concept of the system from Hellstrom's research in order to build a system.

The operation of the system is conceptually illustrated in Figure 27. First, future topographic information is fed to the system from a navigational mapping system. Second, the user sets a target cruise speed and a speed range (or speed window) for the vehicle to operate within. Next, the system generates an optimal plan for throttle, braking levels, and gear selections over a predefined distance. The system then updates these procedures over the entire trip.

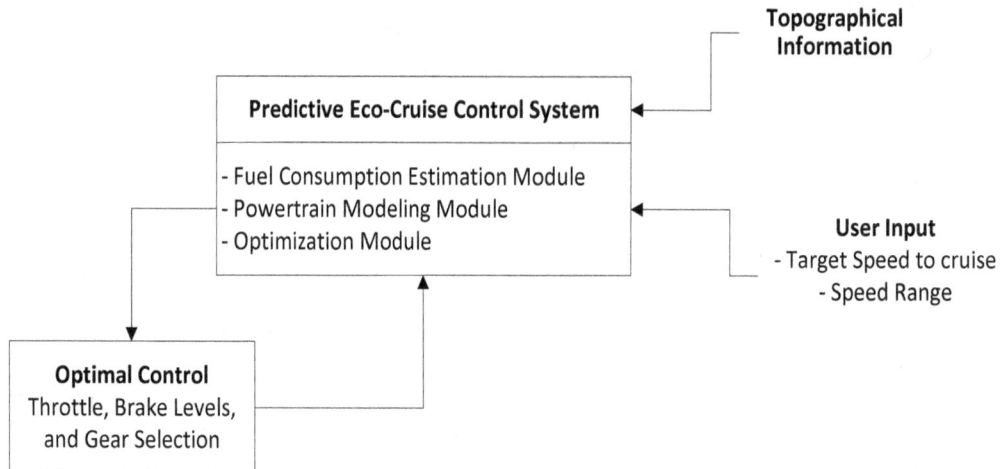

Figure 27: Conceptual Diagram

The predictive ECC system consists of three building blocks: a powertrain module, a fuel consumption module, and an optimization module. These modules are closely connected with each other so that the system can simulate the vehicle operations under the given topographic information and characteristics of a testing vehicle, estimate the fuel consumption rates based on the vehicle operating conditions, and find an optimal control plan that minimizes the vehicle fuel consumption while satisfying the preset minimum vehicle speed levels using the optimization module.

4.1.2 Optimization Module

The optimization module is critical in defining the structure of the system. There are three system parameters used; namely: the unit distance, the optimization look-ahead distance, and the plan implementation distance, as illustrated in Figure 28. The unit distance, the first parameter, is also termed the stage length (d_s). The stage length is the unit of discretization for solving the problem. A vehicle control plan remains constant for the duration of a stage. Any changes in input are made at the stage boundary. The optimization look-ahead distance (d_o), the second parameter, is the distance for which the optimization is performed. Finally, the plan implementation distance (d_f), the last parameter, is the distance for which the optimized plan is implemented. For example, assume that a driver plans a 5-km long trip and defines the stage length, look-ahead distance, and plan implementation distance as 100 m, 1 km, and 500 m, respectively. First, the system discretizes the 5-km long trip at 100 m stage lengths, which results in a 50-stage trip. Then the optimization is carried out every 500 m using the road profile over the next 1 km. In other words, the system calculates the optimal control over from 0 m to 1000 m at the beginning. Next, the system repeats the optimization at 500 m looking ahead from 500 m to 1500 m.

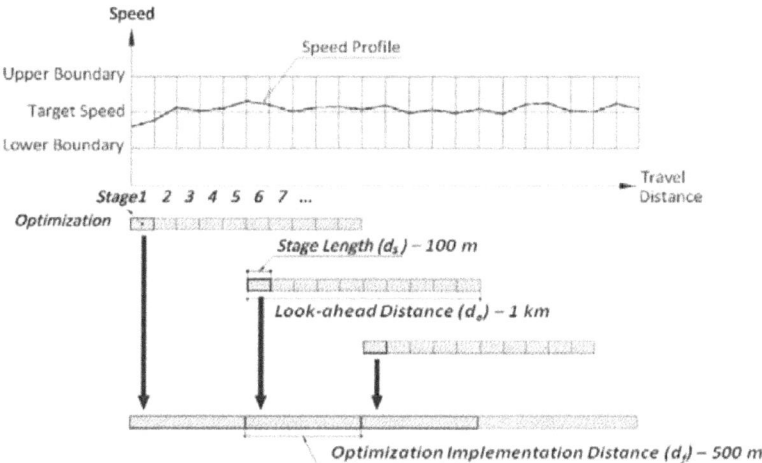

Figure 28: Illustration of Optimization

Each optimization is performed over three steps. In the first step, the search space is defined, which entails determining the range of speed and gear levels which the vehicle is able to achieve based on its performance and the road topographic information. In the second step, the defined search space is discretized to form a state space (where a state is defined by the speed and gear level). Next, a network is constructed by pairing (linking) a state to another state, which represents a transition from one state to another. For example, the transition from the speed of 63 km/h at gear 3 at the end of stage i-1 to a speed of 65 km/h at gear 3 at the beginning of stage i can be represented by linking the two states. Third, all transitions are evaluated with regard to fuel consumption levels and other penalties. In the third step, an optimal control plan (which yields the minimum cost) is searched. The following section describes each step in further detail. It should be noted that the model assumes that transitions from one gear to another occur instantaneously at the stage boundaries and that the changes in speed occur over the stage length.

STEP1: Defining the Search Space

Simulation of the powertrain is required to define the physically achievable search space. In order to conduct the simulation, gear ratio information is required. Given that it is possible that several gears generate an engine speed within the valid engine speed range, the gear that generates the maximum acceleration level is used to define the search space upper boundary of the gear state space. Likewise, the gear that generates the minimum acceleration level is used to define the search space lower boundary. In this study a 1/10 second time step was used as the simulation step size.

In order to determine the maximum speed (V_{sim_max}) at the stage boundary, the simulation is conducted from the initial speed at the maximum throttle, which generates the maximum power. This study assumes 99 percent as the maximum throttle. As illustrated in Figure 29, the user-defined upper (V_{user_max}) and lower (V_{user_low}) speed boundaries are also used to constrain the simulation results. The simulated maximum speed is then compared with the user-defined upper boundary. If the maximum speed is greater than the upper boundary, the search space upper boundary is set to the user-specified upper boundary; otherwise, it is set to the maximum speed. In the next stage, the simulation is conducted from the search space upper boundary of the previous stage. The simulation continues iterating until the user-defined distance is reached in order to define a set of maximum speeds over an optimization.

The search space lower boundary is defined using the same simulation procedures with the minimum throttle level. The minimum throttle level is assumed to be 15 percent. The simulation begins at the initial speed over the first stage. Then the simulated minimum speed (V_{sim_min}) at the end of the first stage is compared with the user-defined lower and upper boundaries to determine the search space lower boundary as follows.

$$V_{low} = \min\left(\max\left(V_{sim\_min}, V_{user\_min} \right), V_{user\_max} \right) \tag{42}$$

In the next stage, the vehicle speed (V^*) at the start of the simulation is determined based on the relationship between the simulated speed (V_{sim_min}), the user-defined target speed (V_{ref}), and the lower boundary (V_{user_min}). If the simulated speed is greater than the target speed, then V^* is set to the target speed. If the simulated speed is less than the lower boundary, then the speed V^* is set to the lower boundary. This ensures that the initial speed is within the user-defined boundary.

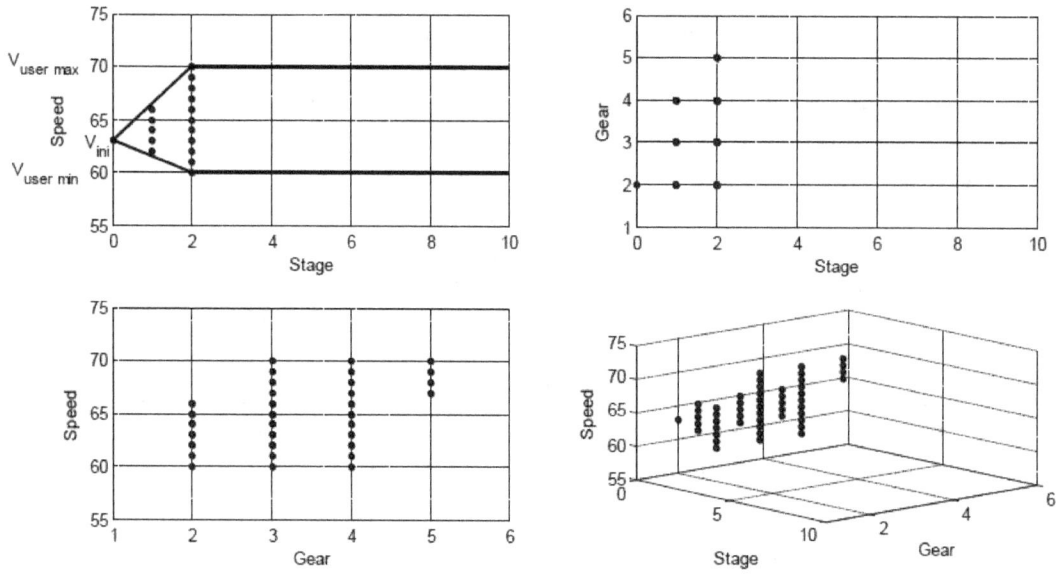

Figure 29: Illustration of Search Space

Given the set of the search space lower and upper boundaries, the search space is discretized at a user-defined increment from the lower to the upper boundary. The study uses 1-km/h as the increment unit. For example, if the boundaries of the first stage are (63, 70) then the speeds of (63, 64, 65, 66, 67, 68, 69, 70) form the search space for the vehicle speed, and a set of possible gears that generate a valid engine speed at each of the speeds is then defined. For example, gears 2, 3, and 4 can be a valid gear set for the speed of 63 km/h if they generate a valid engine speed, which is between the minimum and maximum engine speeds, as illustrated in Figure 29.

STEP2: Building a Network

The next step is connecting a state at the beginning of stage *i* to a state at the end of stage *i*, which means a transition in speed and gear over stage *i*. For example, a potential transition can be described as connecting the state of (63 km/h @ gear 3 at the beginning of stage 1) to the one of (65 km/h @ gear 3 at the end of stage 1). Once all the connections are completed, then a network (also referred to as a graph), which consists of states and connectors, is constructed. The constructed network provides the convenience of easily implementing the shortest path algorithm in the optimization algorithm.

In the course of constructing the network, the transitions need to be evaluated with regard to fuel consumption and other penalties using Equation (43).

$$Cost = w_1 \times FC_{(v_0, v_1)} + w_2 \times \left| \frac{v_1}{v_{ref}} - 1 \right| \times FC_{(v_{ref})} + w_3 \times \left| g_1 - g_0 \right| \times FC_{(v_{ref})} \qquad (43)$$

Where w_1 is the fuel consumption weight factor, w_2 is the speed deviation weight factor, w_3 is the gear change penalty weight factor, v_0 is the initial speed, v_1 is the final speed, v_{ref} is the target speed, g_0 is the initial gear, g_1 is the final gear, $FC_{(v0, v1)}$ is the fuel consumption to accelerate from v_0 to v_1 over the stage length, and $FC_{(vref)}$ is the fuel consumption at v_{ref} over a stage.

The fuel consumption rates are calculated using the VT-CPFM-1 model. For the calculation of fuel consumption rates, the average speed of the two states is used, assuming that the acceleration level remains constant over the stage length. If the difference in the gears over a stage *i* is greater than 1, the penalty is set to infinity in order to avoid unreasonable gear shifts. All the penalties are normalized by multiplying by the fuel consumption rate at the target speed.

STEP3: Finding an Optimal Vehicle Control Set

Step 3 involves exploring the search space to compute an optimal set of vehicle controls. First, this study employs Dijkstra's algorithm that was developed by the Dutch computer scientist Edsger Dijkstra in the late 1950s [52]. It is a graph search algorithm that solves the shortest path problems using shortest path trees. The algorithm finds the minimum cost path from a given source node (state) to every other node, thus it is widely used in routing problems. Given that the structure of the system being discussed here is similar to those of shortest path problems, it is easier to solve these problems using Dijkstra's algorithm. States and transitions in this system can be thought of as nodes (vertices) and edges in shortest path problems.

In addition to Dijkstra's algorithm, a heuristic algorithm was developed as part of the research effort to enhance the execution time with a minimal loss of cost. Although Dijkstra's algorithm provides a good performance for small search space problems, it requires significant computational time to solve large search space problems (such as using longer look-ahead distances and wide speed boundaries). While Dijkstra's algorithm explores all the possible paths, the heuristic algorithm only searches a portion of the paths. The heuristic algorithm starts with the initial speed and finds an optimal solution for the first stage that produces the minimum cost. The solution for the first stage is then fixed and the algorithm starts with the final speed of the first stage and then finds an optimal solution for the second stage. The algorithm repeats this procedure until the final stage. In other words, the procedure finds the minimum for each stage and computes the total minimum as the sum of stage minima. A merit for using the heuristic algorithm is that it is possible to implement a constraint on the frequency of gear shifting to minimize frequent gear shifts. This is possible because it is easy to track the gear changes when using the heuristic algorithm. Specifically, users can specify the minimum number of stages between gear shifts. The algorithm can then ensure that no gear shifts are spaced closer than the user-specified minimum spacing.

4.2 Demonstration of the Predictive Eco-Cruise Control system

For the demonstration of the predictive ECC system, a 2011 Toyota Camry was used in this study. The Toyota Camry has a 2.4 L engine and 8.9 and 13.2 kilometers per liter (21 and 31 MPG) EPA city and highway fuel cycles, respectively. The specifications of the vehicle, which are publicly available, were used to calibrate the fuel consumption and powertrain models. The details of the calibration procedures of the models are available in the literature [53].

The predictive ECC system was simulated on a 45-km section of Interstate 81 from Roanoke to Blacksburg in the state of Virginia. Since the study section includes multiple uphill and downhill segments, with grades ranging from -4 percent to +4 percent (as illustrated in Figure 30), it is appropriate to demonstrate the performance of the system. Specifically, it is possible to examine the behavior of the system on the uphill and downhill sections regarding speed, throttle, braking level, and gear selection. The simulation will show how the system optimizes fuel consumption rates when uphill sections are anticipated in a predictive manner and how the system maximizes the utilization of gravitational energy.

A set of scenarios was prepared for each of the target speeds by varying the speed boundaries as described in Table 15. Given that the majority of the study section has a speed limit of 104 km/h (65 mph), it is reasonable to think that most drivers are likely to drive between 96 km/h (60 mph) and 112 km/h (70 mph) at free-flow traffic conditions. Consequently, three speeds of 96 km/h, 104 km/h, and 112 km/h were used as the target speeds, and the speeds varying ± 8 km/h (5 mph) from the target speeds were used as the lower and upper boundaries for the system. For the system configuration, 100 m, 1000 m, and 1000 m were used as the d_s, d_o, and d_f system parameters, respectively. For the calculation of the cost for the optimization, only the fuel consumption was considered, which means that the weight factors of (w_1=1, w_2=0, w_3=0) were used. Dijkstra's algorithm was used to find the optimal solution in this simulation.

It is worth noting that the predictive ECC system is assumed to have full control of the vehicle. Consequently, the system can save fuel even when the vehicle is cruising at a constant speed because the system can inject the exact amount of fuel needed to maintain the target speed. That is one of the reasons that the fuel efficiencies analyzed in this study are greater than the fuel efficiencies rated by the EPA.

As seen in Table 15, each of the scenario sets has five scenarios that have different speed ranges. The scenario with the speed range of 0 km/h is the baseline (single target speed), which is compared with the other scenarios. Fuel consumption normally increased as the target speed increased. In addition, the fuel savings became larger as the speed range became wider. The simulation results demonstrated that using the predictive ECC system results in significant fuel savings. Specifically, the speed range of ± 8 km/h resulted in fuel savings of up to 15% when compared to the baseline for all of the target speeds. However, the execution time – which is the computational time to optimize the vehicle controls – significantly increased as the speed range became wider because there were significant increases in the number of feasible solutions from the initial state to the final state as the search space was extended.

Table 15: Simulation of Predictive Eco-Cruise Control System Integrated with Dijkstra's Algorithm

Target Speed	Scenario Number	Speed range	Shortest Path Algorithm			
			Fuel Consumed (L)	Fuel Efficiency (Km/L & MPG)	Relative Difference (%) in Fuel Efficiency to the Base Case	Execution Time (min.)
96 km/h (60 mph)	1	0.0 km/h (0.0 mph) (base case)	3.18	14.29 km/h (33.61 MPG)	-	1.7
	2	± 2.0 km/h (1.3 mph)	3.07	14.79 (34.78)	3.5%	5.1
	3	± 4.0 km/h (2.5 mph)	2.98	15.25 (35.86)	6.7%	14.0
	4	± 6.0 km/h (3.8 mph)	2.90	15.68 (36.89)	9.7%	30.0
	5	± 8.0 km/h (5.0 mph)	2.83	16.06 (37.78)	12.4%	53.2
104 km/h (65 mph)	6	0.0 km/h (0.0 mph) (base case)	3.45	13.18 (31.00)	-	1.4
	7	± 2.0 km/h (1.3 mph)	3.32	13.67 (32.15)	3.7%	4.9
	8	± 4.0 km/h (2.5 mph)	3.22	14.13 (33.23)	7.2%	13.8
	9	± 6.0 km/h (3.8 mph)	3.12	14.56 (34.25)	10.5%	27.9
	10	± 8.0 km/h (5.0 mph)	3.03	14.98 (35.24)	13.7%	42.4
112 km/h (70 mph)	11	0.0 km/h (0.0 mph) (base case)	3.78	12.01 (28.26)	-	0.8
	12	± 2.0 km/h (1.3 mph)	3.64	12.47 (29.33)	3.8%	1.7
	13	± 4.0 km/h (2.5 mph)	3.51	12.93 (30.41)	7.6%	5.5
	14	± 6.0 km/h (3.8 mph)	3.40	13.37 (31.44)	11.3%	12.4
	15	± 8.0 km/h (5.0 mph)	3.30	13.76 (32.38)	14.6%	21.8

In Figure 30, the speed, throttle, and fuel consumption profiles are illustrated with the roadway grades. The figure demonstrates that the predictive ECC system makes an effort to maintain the lowest possible speed when the vehicle is running on uphill sections in order to save fuel. Further, the system increases the vehicle speed prior to entering an upgrade section, preparing it for the upcoming climb. Alternatively, the system attempts to maximize the utilization of gravitational energy when the vehicle is running along downhill sections. The fuel savings are clearly seen in the subplot (d) as the vehicle uses the predictive ECC system with different speed ranges.

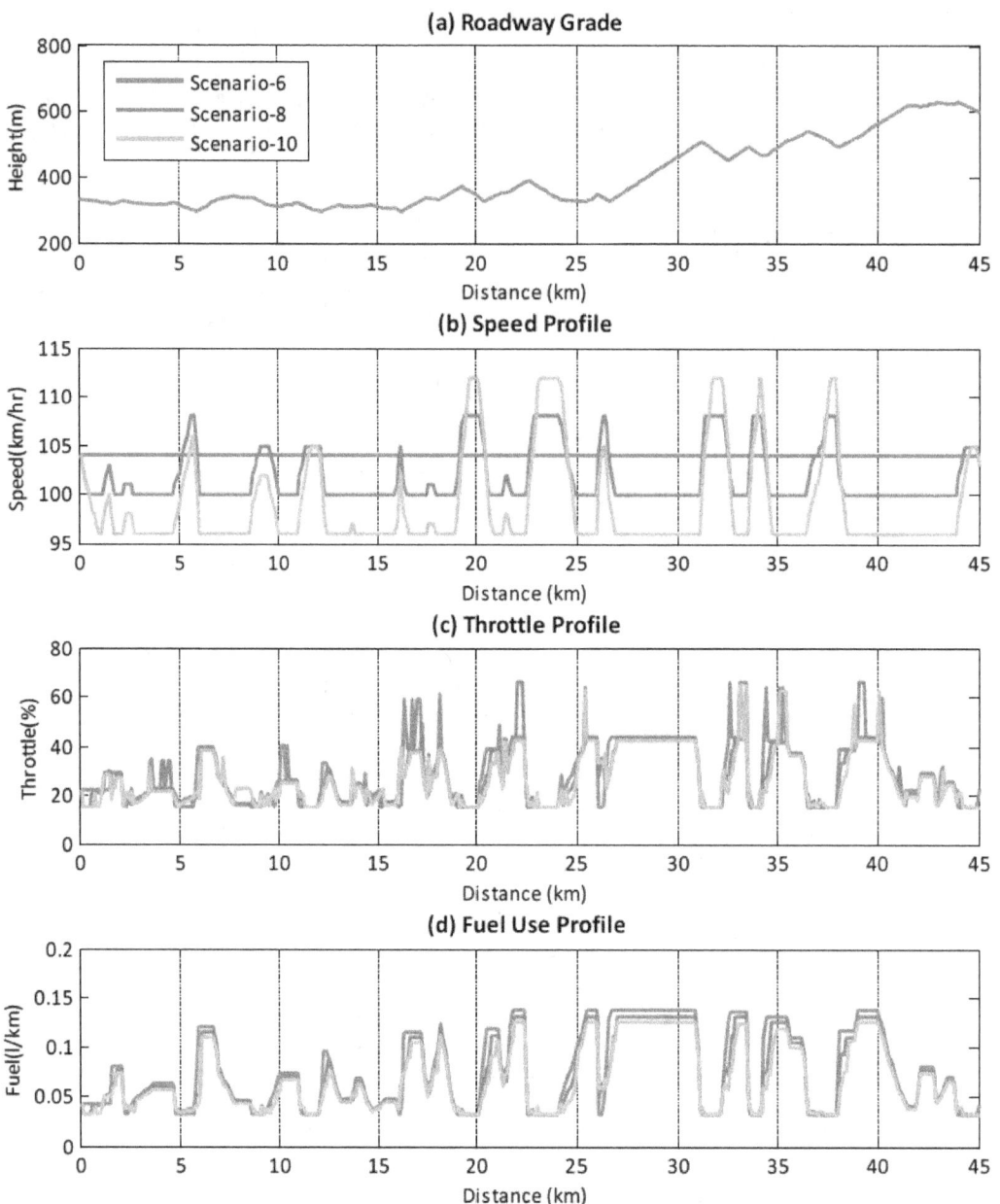

Figure 30: Speed, Throttle, and Fuel Consumption Profiles Along With Topographic Information of the Study Section (Target Speed = 104 km/h)

4.3 Dijkstra's Shortest path vs. Heuristic Algorithm

Although the use of the predictive ECC system integrated with Dijkstra's shortest path algorithm results in significant fuel savings, especially when the vehicle travels on hilly terrains, real applications of the system might be limited because the computational time is not within real time. For instance, the computational time for Scenario-5 (the target speed is 96 km/h and the speed range is ± 8 km/h) for the entire 45km section is 53 minutes, which might be longer than the actual travel time (45 km / 96 km/h = 28 minutes). An optimal vehicle control plan should be provided to either the driver or the vehicle system in a timely manner so that the vehicle can be ready to follow the plan before it reaches the planned sections. The reason for the long computational time is attributed to the fact that Dijkstra's shortest path algorithm finds all the minimum paths from the initial node (state) to the other nodes.

As mentioned earlier, a heuristic algorithm was developed for this research. For comparison purposes, the same scenarios were tested using the predictive ECC system integrated with the heuristic algorithm, as seen in Table 16. The simulation results indicate that the heuristic method significantly improves the computation time but slightly reduces the fuel efficiency (approximately 1 percent). For instance, the differences in the MPG and the Execution Time between both simulations of Scenario-15 are -1.5 and -91.3 percent, respectively. Consequently, it is worthwhile to use the predictive ECC system integrated with the heuristic algorithm.

Table 16: Simulation of Predictive Eco-Cruise Control System Integrated with the Heuristic Algorithm

Target Speed	Scenario Number	Speed range	Fuel Consumed (L)	Fuel Efficiency (Km/L & MPG)	Execution Time (min.)	Relative Difference (%)* to Shortest Path Algorithm	
						Fuel Efficiency	Execution Time
96 km/h (60 mph)	1	0.0 km/h (0.0 mph)	3.19	14.26 (33.53)	1.8	-0.2%	10.9%
	2	± 2.0 km/h (1.3 mph)	3.09	14.7 (34.58)	2.0	-0.6%	-61.3%
	3	± 4.0 km/h (2.5 mph)	3.01	15.11 (35.53)	2.0	-0.9%	-85.8%
	4	± 6.0 km/h (3.8 mph)	2.93	15.5 (36.47)	2.2	-1.1%	-92.7%
	5	± 8.0 km/h (5.0 mph)	2.87	15.85 (37.29)	2.3	-1.3%	-95.6%
104 km/h (65 mph)	6	0.0 km/h (0.0 mph)	3.46	13.13 (30.89)	1.6	-0.4%	10.3%
	7	± 2.0 km/h (1.3 mph)	3.35	13.56 (31.89)	1.7	-0.8%	-66.1%
	8	± 4.0 km/h (2.5 mph)	3.25	13.98 (32.89)	1.7	-1.0%	-87.3%
	9	± 6.0 km/h (3.8 mph)	3.16	14.37 (33.81)	1.9	-1.3%	-93.2%
	10	± 8.0 km/h (5.0 mph)	3.07	14.78 (34.77)	2.1	-1.4%	-95.1%
112 km/h (70 mph)	11	0.0 km/h (0.0 mph)	3.78	12.01 (28.25)	1.2	0.0%	55.4%
	12	± 2.0 km/h (1.3 mph)	3.66	12.4 (29.17)	1.4	-0.5%	-21.4%
	13	± 4.0 km/h (2.5 mph)	3.55	12.8 (30.1)	1.6	-1.0%	-70.7%
	14	± 6.0 km/h (3.8 mph)	3.44	13.23 (31.11)	1.7	-1.0%	-86.0%
	15	± 8.0 km/h (5.0 mph)	3.35	13.56 (31.9)	1.9	-1.5%	-91.3%

4.4 Sensitivity of Weight Factor for Deviation from Target Speed

The demonstration clearly showed that the predictive ECC system maintains the vehicle speed on the lower end of the target range when the vehicle travels on uphill sections. However, some drivers might want to maintain the vehicle speed slightly closer to the target speed even on uphill sections. In order to adjust the system to compromise the fuel efficiency and the deviation from the target speed, the sensitivity of the speed deviation weight factor (w_2) was tested while considering the other weight factors constant ($w_1=1$, $w_3=0$). Specifically, Scenario-10 (Target speed = 104 km/h, Speed range = ± 8 km/h) was used as the sensitivity test scenario. The w_2

weight factor was varied from 0 up to 0.8 in 0.1 increments and each of the results was compared to the baseline, which has the w_2 of 0.0 as seen in Table 17.

The fuel efficiency decreased as the w_2 weight factor increased, as can be seen in Table 17. In particular, the fuel efficiency values remained the same and the speed profiles did not change from the w_2 of 0.3 through 0.8. The vehicle speeds approached the target speed as the w_2 weight factor was increased, as illustrated in Figure 31. Given that the fuel efficiency of Scenario-6 described in Table 16 was 13.13 km/l (30.89 MPG), it could not be expected to show significant fuel savings if a w_2 weight factor greater than 0.3 is used under the given circumstances. Consequently, it is recommended to select a weight factor after a sensitivity test to realize positive fuel savings.

Table 17: Weight Factor (w_2) Sensitivity Test Results

Target Speed	Speed Range	Weight Factor (w_2)	Fuel Consumed (L)	Fuel Efficiency (Km/L & MPG)	Relative Difference (%) to Base Case
104 km/h (65 mph)	± 8.0 km/h (5.0 mph)	0.0 (Base case)	3.07	14.78 km/l (34.77 MPG)	-
		0.1	3.09	14.71 (34.61)	-0.5%
		0.2	3.29	13.81 (32.48)	-6.6%
		0.3	3.45	13.17 (30.99)	-10.9%
		0.4	3.45	13.17 (30.99)	-10.9%
		0.5	3.45	13.17 (30.99)	-10.9%
		0.6	3.45	13.17 (30.99)	-10.9%
		0.7	3.45	13.17 (30.99)	-10.9%
		0.8	3.45	13.17 (30.99)	-10.9%

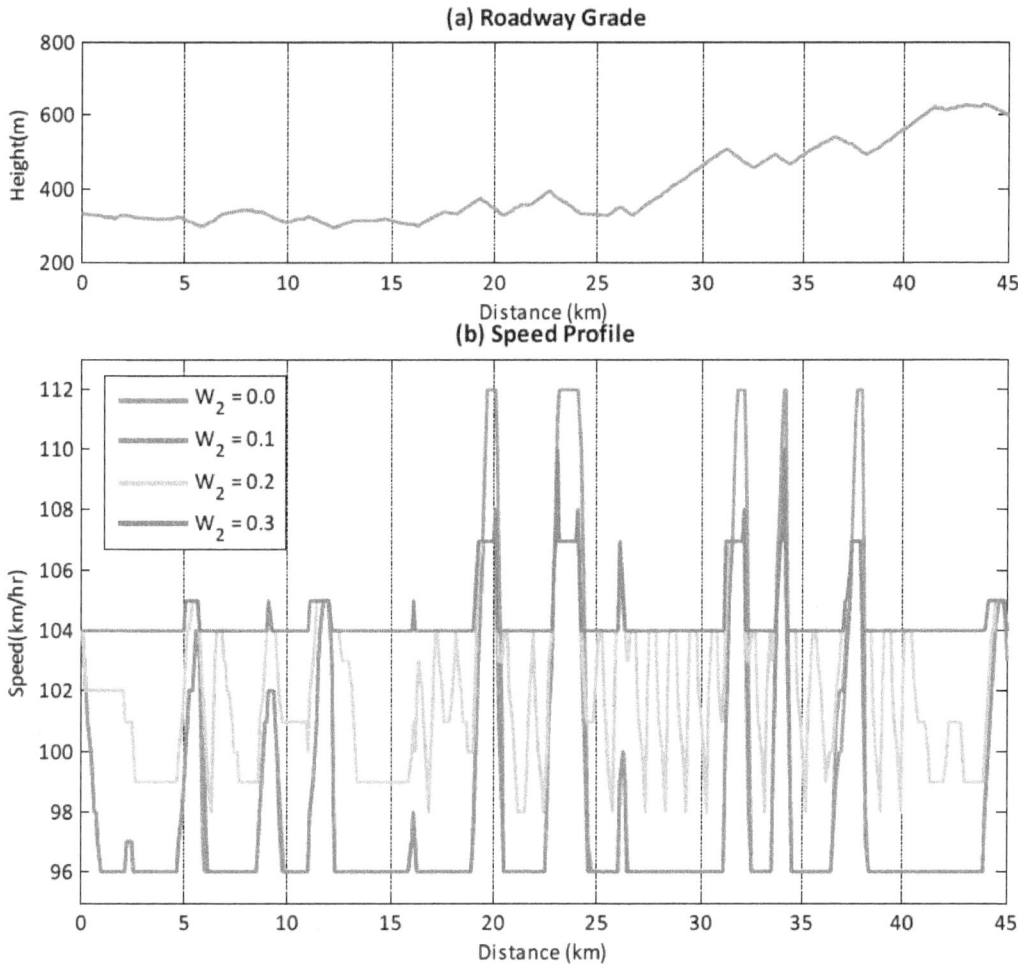

Figure 31: Speed Profiles for Different Weight Factors (w_2)

4.5 Sensitivity to Model Parameters

Given that the system performance regarding the fuel savings and computational times might vary depending on the system parameters (d_s, d_o, and d_f parameters), a sensitivity study was conducted to quantify the relationship between the parameter values from a practical standpoint. For the test, Scenario-10 that is described in Table 15 and Table 16 was used with the set of weight factors of (w_1=1, w_2=0, w_3=0). The d_s parameter was varied from 50 m to 200 m and the d_o and d_f parameters were varied from 500 m up to 3000 m, as demonstrated in Table 18.

In general, the system integrated with the shortest-path algorithm resulted in greater fuel savings when compared to one integrated with the heuristic algorithm. Specifically, the maximal difference in fuel consumption between the two systems was 2.1 percent. However, the heuristic algorithm was found to be significantly superior to the shortest-path algorithm with regard to the execution time. For instance, the execution times were 1103 minutes (18.4 hours) and 15 minutes for Index-7, which has a set of system parameters of (50 m, 3000 m, 500 m), while using the shortest-path algorithm saved 0.06 L more as compared to the heuristic algorithm as seen in Table 18.

Table 18: System Parameter (d_s, d_o, and d_f) Sensitivity Test Results

Index	d_s (m)	d_o (m)	d_f (m)	Shortest-Path Algorithm				Heuristic Algorithm			
				Fuel (l)	Fuel Effi. MPG	Total Exec. Time (min.)	Exec. Time/ Opt. (sec.)	Fuel (l)	MPG	Total Exec. Time (min.)	Exec. Time/ Opt. (sec.)
1	50	500	500	3.08	14.74 (34.67)	55	36.7	3.11	14.62 (34.38)	3	1.7
2		1000	500	3.05	14.90 (35.05)	158	105.4	3.11	14.63 (34.42)	5	3.4
3		1000	1000	3.05	14.88 (34.99)	78	103.4	3.11	14.63 (34.41)	3	3.5
4		2000	500	3.05	14.92 (35.09)	494	329.3	3.11	14.62 (34.40)	10	6.6
5		2000	1000	3.04	14.93 (35.13)	249	331.9	3.11	14.63 (34.42)	5	6.7
6		2000	2000	3.05	14.91 (35.06)	131	350.6	3.10	14.64 (34.44)	3	6.7
7		3000	500	3.05	14.92 (35.09)	1103	735.0	3.11	14.62 (34.40)	15	9.7
8		3000	1000	3.04	14.93 (35.13)	538	717.6	3.11	14.63 (34.41)	7	9.8
9		3000	2000	3.04	14.95 (35.16)	303	807.6	3.10	14.65 (34.45)	4	9.7
10		3000	3000	3.05	14.91 (35.07)	204	817.8	3.10	14.65 (34.45)	3	10.3
11	100	500	500	3.05	14.88 (35.01)	35	23.7	3.07	14.78 (34.76)	2	1.4
12		1000	500	3.03	15.01 (35.29)	94	62.5	3.07	14.78 (34.76)	4	2.8
13		1000	1000	3.03	14.98 (35.24)	47	62.8	3.07	14.78 (34.77)	2	2.8
14		2000	500	3.03	15.01 (35.31)	209	139.0	3.07	14.81 (34.84)	8	5.5
15		2000	1000	3.02	15.03 (35.34)	105	140.6	3.07	14.80 (34.81)	4	5.5
16		2000	2000	3.03	15.00 (35.28)	55	146.8	3.07	14.79 (34.78)	2	5.6
17		3000	500	3.03	15.01 (35.31)	373	248.7	3.07	14.80 (34.81)	12	8.0
18		3000	1000	3.02	15.03 (35.34)	189	252.5	3.07	14.79 (34.78)	6	8.1
19		3000	2000	3.02	15.03 (35.36)	106	282.9	3.07	14.80 (34.80)	3	8.1
20		3000	3000	3.03	15.01 (35.31)	74	294.9	3.07	14.79 (34.79)	2	8.6
21	200	1000	1000	3.03	14.98 (35.25)	34	45.4	3.06	14.86 (34.94)	2	2.4
22		2000	1000	3.03	15.02 (35.33)	74	99.0	3.07	14.81 (34.83)	4	4.9
23		2000	2000	3.03	15.00 (35.27)	39	104.2	3.06	14.86 (34.96)	2	4.7
24		3000	1000	3.03	15.02 (35.33)	121	161.2	3.08	14.73 (34.65)	6	7.4
25		3000	2000	3.02	15.03 (35.35)	65	174.2	3.07	14.81 (34.84)	3	7.4
26		3000	3000	3.03	15.01 (35.30)	44	177.5	3.06	14.85 (34.92)	2	7.4

In terms of the effects of the system parameters, the fuel savings increased as the d_s parameter increased when using both algorithms. These results were different from what was expected since it is reasonable that a shorter d_s would result in greater fuel savings. The results showed that the relationship is not straightforward but complex. It might be related to some other factors such as the quality of the topographic information. Additionally, a longer d_o and a shorter d_f parameter generally resulted in a reduction in fuel consumption levels, although it required more execution times for computing the optimal control plan.

Indices -19 and -23 were the parameter sets that resulted in the best fuel economies when the shortest path and the heuristic algorithms were used, as demonstrated in Table 18. Although they were analyzed as the best sets, the fuel consumption levels were not significantly less than those for other sets. In other words, the variation in the fuel consumption due to changes in the system parameters was not high. The coefficients of variation for the fuel consumption for each algorithm were 0.5 and 0.6 percent, respectively. However, the variation in the execution time was generally high, and higher when the Dijkstra shortest-path algorithm was used. Consequently, it is recommended to select system parameters that are superior with regard to the execution time. For example, indices -11 or -21 can be a good set because these showed a fast execution speed and a good efficiency when compared to the other parameter sets.

4.6 Conclusions

The research presented here developed a predictive ECC system, integrating the previously developed fuel consumption model and the powertrain model, to save fuel while maintaining the vehicle speed within a user-specified window. The study demonstrated that the developed predictive ECC system can generate an optimal vehicle control plan in real time. In addition, the study demonstrated that the heuristic search algorithm finds the optimum plan more quickly with a gap in the objective function of less than 1 percent when compared to the shortest path algorithm. Specifically, testing of the system showed that the largest fuel savings are achieved along hilly terrain sections. In addition, the study demonstrated that the penalty for the deviation from the target speed is used to control the degree of the deviation. For the selection of system parameters, it is recommended to select those that are superior with regard to the execution time because the system parameters do not significantly affect the optimum solution as much as the execution time.

For future research efforts, there is a need to quantify the potential benefits of using the predictive ECC system in a systematic manner. It would be especially insightful to compare the performance of the predictive ECC system with that of the conventional CC system.

5. POTENTIAL BENEFITS OF PREDICTIVE ECO-CRUISE CONTROL SYSTEMS

This section investigates the potential benefits of the developed predictive ECC system. In the previous section, the predictive ECC system was tested on a limited section of highway to demonstrate that the system is fully functional and also develop an optimal system parameter set that is used to configure the optimization procedures. Consequently, there is a need to evaluate the predictive ECC system in a comprehensive manner in order to fully quantify the potential benefits of the predictive ECC system.

The objective of this section is to quantify the potential benefits of the system considering the variations in vehicle types and roadway grades when compared to the conventional CC system. This section also investigates the potential benefits for the entire United States. Finally, the study quantifies the fuel-saving benefits of using the predictive ECC over a New York City to Los Angeles route.

5.1 Conventional Cruise Control Operations

In order to quantify the potential benefit of using the predictive ECC system, this section first introduces traditional CC operations that were developed in a previous study [54] on hilly terrain roadways.

In order to characterize the operation of conventional CC systems, a passenger car (a 2005 Cadillac STS) was driven on a section of Interstate 81 in the state of Virginia while the conventional CC was activated. The study section runs from Roanoke, VA (milepost 143) to Christiansburg, VA (milepost 118) and is 45 km (28.1 mi) in length. The roadway grade ranges from -4 percent to +4 percent. The test vehicle had a 3.6L, V-6 engine with an electronic 5-speed automatic overdrive transmission.

The majority of the test section had a speed limit of 96 km/h (60 mph) or 104 km/h (65 mph). The driver was directed to cruise at the speed limit of the test section and the data were recorded using an OBD II data logger (as illustrated in Figure 32). The CC portion with the target speed of 104 km/h was extracted from the collected data in order to capture the variation in the control. From the extracted data, a speed variation of 1.5 percent was identified between the preset speed and actual cruise speeds. As can be seen in Figure 32, there were oscillations in the speed profiles because the closed-loop CC system attempted to maintain the preset target speed.

Given the analyzed characteristics of the conventional CC system, a simulation module for the conventional CC operations was developed in order to compare it with the predictive ECC operation. The vehicle powertrain model, which is integrated with the predictive system, is also used for the simulation of vehicle movement. The system was designed to control the throttle or brake level to maintain its preset target speed within a speed range of 1.5 percent under the given topographic information. Specifically, if the current speed of a vehicle is higher than its target speed, then the minimal throttle level is applied. On the other hand, if the speed of a vehicle is lower than the target speed, then the vehicle is gradually accelerated. The level of acceleration is determined based on the difference between the vehicle speed and the target speed. Consequently, a greater difference leads to a higher acceleration level.

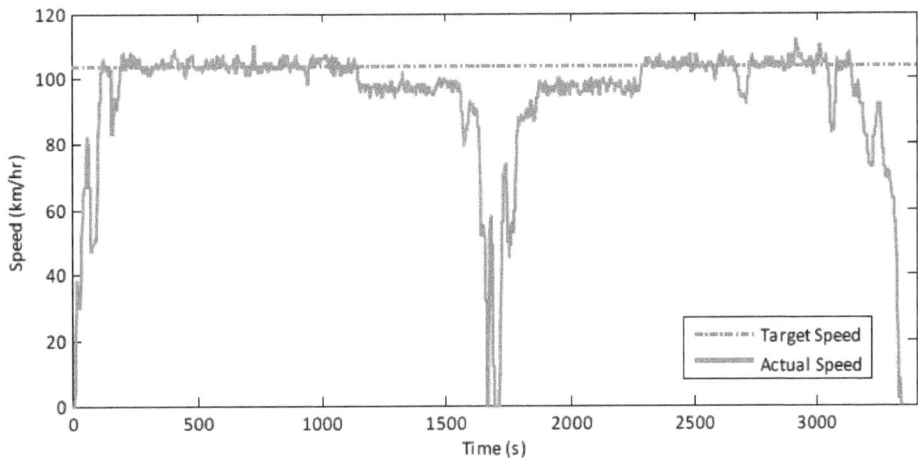

Figure 32: Traditional Cruise Control Operation along I-81 Test Section

5.2 Potential Benefits of Predictive Eco-Cruise Control System

5.2.1 Potential Benefits of an NYC to LA Route

For the demonstration of the predictive ECC system on a real roadway, this section investigates the possible fuel savings of an artificial trip from New York City (NYC), NY to Los Angeles (LA), CA when a driver uses the predictive ECC for the entire trip. The trip starts from the intersection of Chambers St. and Broadway in Manhattan, NY and finishes at the intersection of West 1st St. and North Broadway in Los Angeles, CA. The entire route, 4464 km (or 2790 mi), is mostly highway sections except for a few hundred meters which were required to access from/to the origin and the destination. Figure 33 illustrates the map of the NYC to LA route which utilizes major U.S. highways such as I-80, I-76, I-70, I-15, and I-10. In order to simplify the simulation process, two major assumptions were made during the simulation runs. First, the study assumes that there is no interaction with other vehicles during the trip. Thus, the test vehicles use the predictive ECC mode for the entire trip. Consequently, this represents the upper bound of the potential benefits. Second, the predictive ECC uses the target speed of 104 km/h (65 mph) for the entire route in order to simplify the simulation setting.

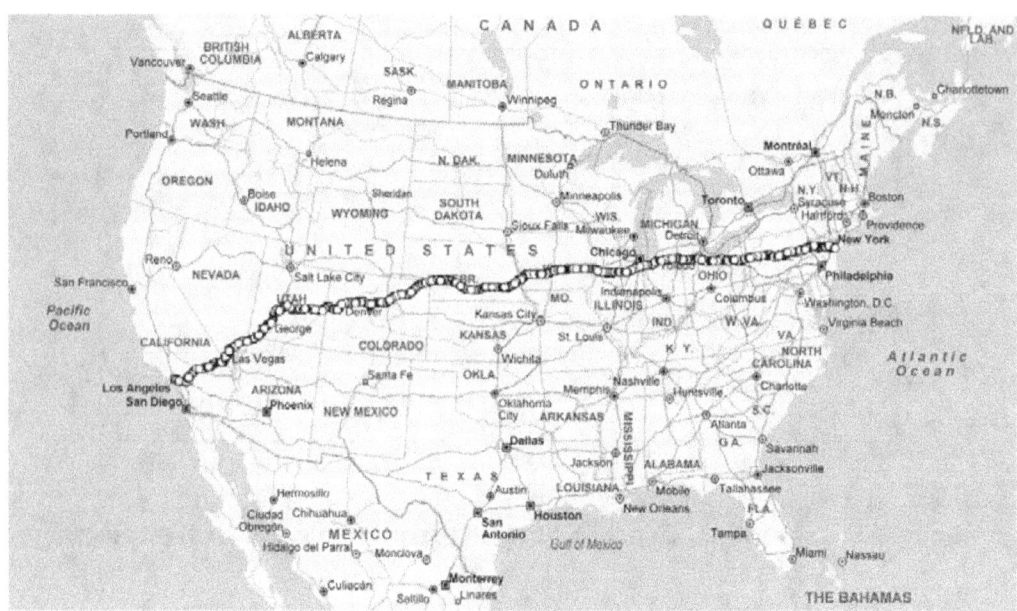

Figure: 33 NYC to LA Route

Table 19 demonstrates the simulation results of a trip from New York City to Los Angeles. Both conventional CC and predictive ECC scenarios were simulated using the MATLAB computing environment. Six test vehicles are selected for the study including four passenger cars and two light-duty trucks: a 2011 Ford F150, a 2011 Toyota Corolla, a 2009 Toyota Camry, a 2008 Chevy Tahoe, a 2007 Chevy Malibu, and a 2008 Chevy Malibu Hybrid. The Chevy Tahoe, Chevy Malibu, Malibu Hybrid, and Toyota Camry are the same vehicles that were utilized in the previous sections. The Ford F150 and the Toyota Corolla were added to the fleet since the F150 was the best-selling truck in the 2011 U.S. market and Toyota Corolla was the best-selling small-size sedan in the 2011 U.S. market.

Table 19: Fuel Savings of the NYC to LA Trip

	Conventional CC		Predictive ECC		Fuel savings
	Fuel (l)	Fuel Economy (km/l - MPG)	Fuel (l)	Fuel Economy (km/l - MPG)	
Toyota Camry	252.8	17.6 (41.9)	227.2	19.7 (46.7)	10.1%
Chevy Malibu	271.3	16.5 (39.1)	241.7	18.5 (43.9)	10.9%
Malibu Hybrid	291.3	15.3 (36.4)	258.5	17.3 (41.0)	11.3%
Chevy Tahoe	469.3	9.5 (22.6)	387.1	11.5 (27.4)	17.5%
Ford F150	473.2	9.4 (22.4)	410.7	10.9 (25.8)	13.2%
Toyota Corolla	232.7	19.2 (45.6)	211.6	21.1 (50.1)	9.1%
Average	**331.8**	**14.6 (34.7)**	**289.5**	**16.5 (39.15)**	**12.0%**

The table demonstrates fuel consumption and fuel economy results of conventional CC and predictive ECC operations when the test vehicles travel the NYC to LA route. The target speed was set to 104 km/h (65 km/h) with a maximum speed of 112 km/h (70 mph) and a minimum speed of 96 km/h (60 mph) for the entire NYC to LA route. The table shows that heavy and large vehicles such as the Chevy Tahoe and Ford F150 consume as much as twice the fuel than a Toyota Corolla does for the conventional CC operational trip. It is noted that the fuel economy data of the conventional CC operations are higher than the EPA fuel economy data. For instance, in case of the 2011 Toyota Camry, the highway fuel economy rating is 33 MPG while the fuel economy of the simulation results is 41.9 MPG. It should be noted that the results of the conventional CC were simulated with a target speed of 104 km/h (65 mph) without any major speed variations. Thus, the simulated fuel economy should be expected to be better than typical driving conditions. Furthermore, the current highway EPA fuel economy rating is equivalent to 47 MPG for the pre-2008 highway EPA fuel economy rating.

The average fuel savings using the predictive ECC mode is 12 percent compared to the conventional CC operated trips. Heavier vehicles such as the Chevy Tahoe and the Ford F150 save more fuel than the other vehicles when vehicles adopt the predictive ECC system. In particular, the Chevy Tahoe and the Ford F150 reduce the fuel consumption by 82 and 63 L of gasoline, respectively, while the Toyota Corolla saves 21 L of fuel over the entire NYC to LA route. The total fuel savings of the Chevy Tahoe and the Ford F150 over the NYC to LA route are equivalent to 17.5 percent and 13.2 percent, respectively, of the total fuel consumption of the conventional CC operated trips.

Table 20 demonstrates the CO_2 emission savings associated with a predictive ECC system over the NYC to LA trip. The predictive ECC trips significantly decrease the CO_2 emissions compared to the conventional CC trips. Also, similar to the fuel consumption results, the Chevy Tahoe and the Ford F150 produce more GHG emission reductions compared to other vehicles. Since the fuel consumption rate is proportional to the CO_2 emission rate, the percentages of relative CO_2 savings are same as those of the fuel savings.

Table 20: CO_2 Savings of the NYC to LA Trip

	Conventional CC CO_2	Predictive ECC CO_2	CO_2 Saving
Toyota Camry	564	507	10%
Malibu	605	539	11%
Malibu Hybrid	650	576	11%
Chevy Tahoe	1047	863	18%
Ford F150	1055	916	13%
Toyota Corolla	519	472	9%
Average	**740**	**646**	**12%**

Table 21 summarizes the simulation results for travel time, average speed, and speed variation for both conventional and predictive ECC trips over the NYC to LA route. The results demonstrate that the usage of the predictive ECC system reduces the average speed of the trip from 103.4 km/h to 97.1 km/h. The average speed of 97.1 km/h is very close to the lower boundary speed (96 km/h) of the predictive ECC system since the predictive ECC system tries to maintain the lower boundary speed as much as possible in order to minimize fuel consumption. Also, the table demonstrates that the lower average speed of the predictive ECC mode increases the total travel time for the NYC to LA trip. Specifically, when vehicles utilize the predictive ECC mode the average travel time increases from 43 to 46 hours. The increased travel time represents a 7-percent increase in travel time. In summary, on average, using the proposed ECC settings saves a vehicle 12 percent in fuel usage but at the same time increases its travel time by 7 percent.

Table 21: Travel Time Increase of the NYC to LA Trip

	Conventional CC			Predictive ECC			Travel Time Increase
	Travel Time (Hr)	Average Speed (km/h)	Standard Deviation Speed (km/h)	Travel Time (Hr)	Average Speed (km/h)	Standard Deviation Speed (km/h)	
Toyota Camry	43.0	103.8	1.1	46.0	97.1	3.1	7.0%
Malibu	43.0	103.7	1.0	46.2	96.8	2.5	7.4%
Malibu Hybrid	43.0	103.8	1.0	46.2	96.6	2.3	7.4%
Chevy Tahoe	42.9	104.0	1.4	46.3	96.5	1.9	7.9%
Ford F150	43.1	103.5	1.1	45.5	98.2	4.2	5.6%
Toyota Corolla	43.0	103.7	1.0	45.9	97.3	3.3	6.7%
Average	**43.0**	**103.8**	**1.1**	**46.0**	**97.1**	**2.9**	**7.0%**

The predictive ECC trips reduced the fuel consumption but increased the travel time significantly. The main reason for the increased travel times is the lowered average speed of the predictive ECC trips. Thus, Table 22 investigated the impacts of the speed deviation weight factor to reduce the speed variation from the target speed (104 km/h) during the NYC to LA trip. The Toyota Camry was utilized for the study. Three speed weight factors of 0.25, 0.50, and 0.75 were introduced to evaluate the impact of the weight factors. The table demonstrates that, in general, as the weight factor increases, the fuel efficiency decreases and the vehicle speed increases. With a weight of 0.25 the travel speed approaches the target speed. The study found that using a weight factor significantly decreases speed variations, with positive fuel savings in the range of 2.2 to 3.5 percent.

Table 22: Impacts of Weight Factor (Toyota Camry)

	Fuel (l)	Fuel Economy (km/l - MPG)	Fuel Saving	Travel Time (Hr)	Average Speed (km/h)	Standard Deviation Speed (km/h)	Travel Time Increase
Conventional CC	252.8	17.5		43.0	103.8	1.1	
Predictive ECC	227.2	19.5	10.1%	46.0	97.1	3.1	7.0%
0.50 Speed Factor	246.8	17.9	2.4%	42.9	104.2	0.8	-0.3%
0.75 Speed Factor	247.2	17.9	2.2%	42.7	104.5	0.8	-0.7%
0.25 Speed Factor	244.0	18.1	3.5%	43.0	103.7	1.0	0.1%

Table 23: Simulation Results of the NYC to LA Route

	Fuel (l)	Fuel Economy (km/l - MPG)	Fuel Savings	Travel Time (Hr)	Average Speed (km/h)	Standard Deviation Speed (km/h)	Travel Time Increase
Toyota Camry							
Conventional CC	252.8	17.5(41.9)		43.0	103.8	1.1	
Predictive ECC (+8 and -8 km/h range)	227.2	19.5(46.7)	10.1%	46.0	97.1	3.1	7.0%
Conventional CC (Target: 97.1 km/h)	239.2	18.5(44.3)	5.4%	45.1	96.9	1.0	4.8%
Predictive ECC (+8 and -1.6 km/h range)	239.6	18.4(44.3)	5.2%	43.3	103.0	1.9	0.8%
Chevy Tahoe							
Conventional CC	469.3	9.4(22.6)		42.9	104.0	1.4	
Predictive ECC (+8 and -8 km/h range)	387.1	11.4(27.4)	17.5%	46.3	96.5	1.9	7.9%
Conventional CC (Target: 96.5 km/h)	431.4	10.2(24.6)	8.1%	45.9	97.3	1.7	6.9%
Predictive ECC (+8 and -1.6 km/h range)	423.7	10.4(25.0)	9.7%	43.5	102.6	1.1	1.4%
Chevy Malibu							
Conventional CC	271.3	16.3(39.1)		43.0	103.7	1.0	
Predictive ECC (+8 and -8 km/h range)	241.7	18.3(43.9)	10.9%	46.2	96.8	2.5	7.4%
Conventional CC (Target: 96.8 km/h)	253.8	17.4(41.8)	6.5%	46.3	96.5	1.0	7.7%
Predictive ECC (+8 and -1.6 km/h range)	256.4	17.2(41.4)	5.5%	43.4	102.8	1.6	1.0%
Malibu Hybrid							
Conventional CC	291.3	15.2(36.4)		43.0	103.8	1.0	
Predictive ECC (+8 and -8 km/h range)	258.5	17.1(41.0)	11.3%	46.2	96.6	2.3	7.4%
Conventional CC (Target: 96.6 km/h)	275.1	16.1(38.5)	5.6%	46.4	96.3	1.0	7.9%
Predictive ECC (+8 and -1.6 km/h range)	274.0	16.1(38.7)	6.0%	43.4	102.8	1.5	0.9%
Ford F150							
Conventional CC	473.2	9.3(22.4)		43.1	103.5	1.1	
Predictive ECC (+8 and -8 km/h range)	410.7	10.8(25.8)	13.2%	45.5	98.2	4.2	5.6%
Conventional CC (Target: 98.2 km/h)	439.9	10.0(24.1)	7.0%	45.6	97.9	1.0	5.8%
Predictive ECC (+8 and -1.6 km/h range)	441.5	10.0(24.0)	6.7%	43.1	103.6	2.6	0.0%
Toyota Corolla							
Conventional CC	232.7	19.0(45.6)		43.0	103.7	1.0	
Predictive ECC (+8 and -8 km/h range)	211.6	20.9(50.1)	9.1%	45.9	97.3	3.3	6.7%
Conventional CC (Target: 97.3 km/h)	218.4	20.2(48.5)	6.1%	46.0	97.0	0.9	7.0%
Predictive ECC (+8 and -1.6 km/h range)	221.7	19.9(47.8)	4.7%	43.3	103.2	2.1	0.7%

Table 23 demonstrates two simulation results: the impacts of using a lower target speed for conventional CC trips, and a different speed range for the predictive ECC trips. The simulation results of the conventional CC trips with a lower target speed are compared to the results of the predictive ECC with a speed range of ± 8 km/h. For instance, in the case of the Chevy Malibu, when the target speed was set to 104 km/h, the predictive ECC trip with a speed range of ± 8 km/h reduced the average speed to 96.8 km/h and saves 10.9 percent of total energy consumption. Thus, in order to compare to the performance of the predictive ECC trip, the conventional CC trip with a target speed of 96.8 km/h was simulated. The table demonstrates that the conventional CC trip with the lowered target speed consumed 253.8 L of fuel with an average speed of 96.5 km/h and a standard deviation of 1.0 km/h. The result confirms that the predictive ECC trips still significantly improve the vehicle fuel efficiency compared to the conventional CC trip with the similar average speed. Specifically, the Malibu with predictive ECC system (average speed: 96.8 km/h) can save 12.1 L of gasoline compared to the conventional CC trip with a similar average speed (96.5 km/h) over the NYC to LA trip. It is interesting to note that, in general, as the speed variation increases, the fuel efficiency of the trip decreases. However, the table demonstrates that the predictive ECC trips experience higher speed fluctuations compared to the conventional CC trips but the predictive ECC trips also use significantly less fuel during the NYC to LA trip.

The study also examines the impacts of using a different speed range for the predictive ECC trips as demonstrated in Table 23. In particular, the predictive ECC mode with +8 km/h and -1.6 km/h is investigated in order to increase the average speed of the NYC to LA trip. The table shows that the predictive ECC trips with the new speed boundary considerably increase the average speeds of the trips, which are very similar to those of the conventional CC trips. For example, when a Chevy Malibu utilized the predictive ECC system with a speed range of +8 and -1.6 km/h, the vehicle saves 5.5 percent of fuel (or 15 L) with a 1-percent increase in the total travel time compared to the conventional CC trip. Similarly, the other five test vehicles saved fuel consumption in the range of 4.7 to 6.7 percent without significantly increasing the travel time (between 0.0 and 1.4 percent increase) when an ECC system with a +8 and -1.6 km/h speed range were utilized. The simulation results demonstrate that the introduction of a different speed range scheme can significantly improve the performance of the system, enhancing vehicle fuel efficiency without increasing the total travel time.

5.2.2 Potential Benefits of a section of Interstate 81

This section investigates the potential benefits on a hilly roadway section. A trip was simulated along a section of Interstate 81 in the state of Virginia that was described in the earlier section. The study section contains the maximum grade of 4 percent and the maximum downhill grade of 5 percent with an average grade of 0.6 percent. For the test, five vehicles were selected from the top 10 best-selling vehicles in the 2010 U.S. market, and a mini-van was added to this group in order to represent different types of vehicles with regard to engine size. The vehicles used in the study were: Ford F150, Toyota Camry, Honda Accord, Toyota Corolla, Honda CR-V, and Toyota Sienna. Given the specifications of each test vehicle, the fuel consumption and powertrain models were calibrated.

Because the majority of the test section had a speed limit of 104 km/h (65 mph), the target speed of the predictive ECC system was set to 104 km/h with the speed range of ± 8 km/h. The study also investigates the predictive ECC mode with +8 km/h and -1.6 km/h. The simulation results were compared with regard to fuel efficiency as described in Table 24.

The test results demonstrated that the fuel savings resulting from the use of the predictive ECC system are significant when compared to the use of the conventional system. Specifically, the average fuel efficiency improvement of the predictive ECC system with the speed range of ± 8 km/h was 17 percent. However, the table also demonstrates that the usage of the predictive ECC system with the speed range of ± 8 km/h reduces the average speed of the trip from 103.8 km/h to 97.7 km/h on average, which is a speed reduction of 5.8 percent. The average speed of 97.7 km/h is very close to the lower boundary speed (96 km/h) of the predictive ECC system.

Similar to the analysis of the NYC to LA trip, the study also examined the effectiveness of the predictive ECC mode with +8 km/h and -1.6 km/h. The table shows when test vehicles utilized the predictive ECC system with a speed range of +8 and -1.6 km/h, the fuel efficiency was increased by 9.0 percent on average with less than a 1-percent speed changes compared to the conventional CC trip. In particular, all six test vehicles saved fuel consumption in the range of 6.1 to 15.1 percent without significantly increasing the travel time. The Ford F150 achieved the most fuel saving: the fuel efficiency increased by 15.1 percent. On the other hand, the Corolla was found to be the vehicle with the least fuel saving among the test vehicles. The study found that heavy vehicles (e.g. Ford F150) can generally achieve more fuel savings when compared to light vehicles (e.g. Toyota Corolla). Similar to the NYC to LA trip case, the simulation results demonstrate that the ECC system with a +8 and -1.6 km/h speed range can significantly improve the performance of the system without reducing the vehicle average speed.

Table 24: I-81 Test Results

Vehicle	Conventional CC		Predictive ECC (± 8 km/h)		Predictive ECC (+8&-1.6 km/h)		Fuel Saving (%)		Speed Reduction (%)	
	Fuel Efficiency Km/l (MPG)	Average Speed (km/h)	Fuel Efficiency Km/l (MPG)	Average Speed (km/h)	Fuel Efficiency Km/l (MPG)	Average Speed (km/h)	Pred. ECC (± 8 km/h)	Pred. ECC (+8 &-1.6 km/h)	Pred. ECC (± 8 km/h)	Pred. ECC (+8 &-1.6 km/h)
Camry	15.3(36.3)	103.6	17.5(41.6)	98.5	16.4(38.9)	103.8	14.5%	7.0%	4.9%	-0.2%
Corolla	15.9(37.9)	103.5	18.0(42.7)	98.3	16.9(40.2)	103.7	12.8%	6.1%	5.1%	-0.1%
Accord	15.4(36.7	103.7	17.8(42.2)	97.6	16.7(39.7)	103.3	15.1%	8.3%	5.9%	0.3%
CRV	12.0(28.5)	103.7	14.0(33.2)	97.0	13.0(30.8)	102.9	16.5%	8.0%	6.4%	0.7%
F150	6.7(16.0)	104.3	8.5(20.2)	97.6	7.8(18.4)	103.3	25.9%	15.1%	6.5%	0.9%
Sienna	11.1(26.3)	103.7	13.0(31.0)	97.5	12.1(28.7)	103.3	17.8%	9.3%	6.0%	0.3%
Average	12.7(30.3)	103.8	14.8(35.1)	97.7	13.8(32.8)	103.4	17.1%	9.0%	5.8%	0.3%

5.3 Estimation of Potential Annual Benefits across the United State

This section investigates potential annual benefits across the United State assuming all vehicles use the predictive ECC system with a speed range of +8 and -1.6 km/h. The accurate quantification of the potential benefits of an area of interest requires extensive efforts to collect relevant data sets such as vehicle fleet composition, traffic condition by the time of day, and vehicle-miles traveled (VMT) by road functional class. The benefit depends on the quality of the collected data sets. For example, suppose that the distribution of roadway grades is the single data set available in the area. The distribution is different from detailed roadway profiles. Designing synthetic roadway profiles, which follow the distribution, is one of the ways to represent the terrain of the area.

Given that the available data resources listed above were very limited, the potential annual benefits across the United States were roughly estimated. The objective of this benefit estimation was to provide insights into the potential fuel savings and the effect that terrains have on the savings. The procedures to calculate the potential benefits can be briefly described in a few steps. First, virtual roadway sections were designed and constructed so that they can represent different terrains. Specifically, three sets of roadway profiles were created based on the previously developed terrain scenarios. A trip was simulated along the constructed profiles once with the conventional system and once with the predictive system by using the six test vehicles that were used in the demonstration. The target speed of the simulation was varied from 72 km/h (45 mph) to 120 km/h (75 mph) in order to cover typical operations in urban and rural roadways. Based on national transportation statistics [55], the composite vehicle fuel consumption rates were calculated using the simulated fuel consumption rates of the test vehicles. Finally, the total fuel consumption was calculated by multiplying the fuel consumption rates and the U.S. VMT statistics [55].

5.3.1 Scenario and Roadway Profile Development

Three topography scenarios were created in order to provide insights into the effect of different terrains on overall fuel savings. The distribution of roadway grades for the three scenarios is summarized in Table 25. Scenarios 1, 2, and 3 were designed to represent three types of terrains in the United States. Specifically, Scenario-3 was generated using the roadway terrains in the states of Washington and Oregon and, thus, these numbers represent a hillier terrain compared to other states in the United States.

Table 25: Proposed Topography Scenarios

Grade	Relative Frequency (%)		
	Scenario-1	Scenario-2	Scenario-3
0%	60%	45%	30%
1%	15%	20%	25%
2%	12%	17%	20%
3%	10%	12%	15%
4%	2%	3%	5%
5%	1%	2%	3%
6%	0%	1%	2%
Sum	100%	100%	100%

Given the proposed distributions, a total of 10 random realizations of 100-km roadway profiles were created for each scenario in order to quantify the effects of different combinations of roadway grades. In creating a profile, a sinusoidal wave for each grade bin (from 0 to 6 percent) was created, which was used to construct the 16-km synthetic roadway profiles. The profile was then created using a set of 100 random numbers to align a total of 100 1-km sinusoidal waves based on the desired distribution for each scenario. The profile for Scenario-3 consists of more high-grade sinusoidal waves when compared to the other profiles.

5.3.2 Simulation Design and Results

As mentioned earlier, the target speed was varied from 72 km/h (45 mph) to up to 120 km/h (75 mph) in 8 km/h increments because it was assumed that those target speeds cover the operations on four roadway types: urban interstates, urban arterials, rural interstates, and rural arterials.

These four roadway types were selected because they are the functional classes employed in the national transportation statistics. For each target speed, each of the vehicles was then simulated on the 10 roadway profiles for each scenario, considering when an ECC system with a +8 and -1.6 km/h speed range is utilized.

In order to take the entire U.S. vehicle fleet composition into account in the potential benefit estimation, the simulated fuel consumption rates of the six test vehicles were mixed together based on the national transportation statistics for 2008 [55]. Specifically, a number of passenger cars and other two-axle 4-tire vehicles were used in the calculation of fleet composition. (Note that vehicles that have more than two axles were not considered in the calculation.) Given that 137,079,843 passenger cars and 101,234,849 other two-axle vehicles were registered in 2008, passenger cars and other vehicles account for 57.5 and 42.5 percent, respectively, of the two-axle vehicles registered in the United States. Consequently, an assumption was made that the passenger cars (which include Toyota Camry, Toyota Corolla, and Honda Accord) all combined account for 57.5 percent, with each passenger car accounting for 19.2 percent of the total fleet. Similarly, Honda CR-V, Toyota Sienna, and Ford F150 were each assumed to account for 14.2 percent of the total fleet.

The mean fuel and MPG estimates are summarized in Table 26. The variation in the fuel use due to the 10 100-km roadway profiles was not significant. All the coefficients of variation values were less than 1 percent when the predictive system was engaged, and 90 percent of the values were less than 2 percent when the conventional system was activated. The simulation results indicated that the fuel consumption generally increased when the vehicle traveled in hillier terrains, such as in Scenario-3. For instance, the fuel consumption of Scenario-3 for the target speed of 80 km/h was 0.3 liters greater than that of Scenario-1 when the conventional CC system was used. As the target speed was varied, the fuel consumption levels changed. Specifically, the vehicle showed the best performance with regard to fuel consumption at the target speed of 72 km/h.

Table 26: Simulation Results on 100-km Roadway Profiles

Scenario	Speed (km/h)	Conventional CC		Predictive ECC (+8 and -1.6 km/h range)		Fuel savings
		Fuel l/100 km (gal/100 km)	Fuel Efficiency km/l (MPG)	Fuel l/100 km (gal/100 km)	Fuel Efficiency km/l (MPG)	
1	72	5.0 (1.3)	21.2 (50.4)	4.9 (1.3)	21.4 (50.8)	1.94%
	80	5.1 (1.3)	20.8 (49.4)	5.1 (1.3)	20.8 (49.3)	0.66%
	88	5.4 (1.4)	19.7 (46.8)	5.3 (1.4)	19.9 (47.2)	2.63%
	96	6.0 (1.6)	18.0 (42.8)	5.7 (1.5)	18.6 (44.2)	4.41%
	104	6.6 (1.7)	16.2 (38.5)	6.2 (1.6)	17.2 (40.9)	6.81%
	112	7.4 (1.9)	14.7 (34.9)	6.9 (1.8)	15.7 (37.3)	7.16%
	120	8.3 (2.2)	13.2 (31.3)	7.7 (2.0)	14.2 (33.6)	7.58%
2	72	5.1 (1.3)	20.7 (49.1)	5.0 (1.3)	20.8 (49.3)	1.64%
	80	5.3 (1.4)	20.2 (48.0)	5.2 (1.4)	20.3 (48.1)	0.71%
	88	5.6 (1.5)	19.1 (45.4)	5.4 (1.4)	19.4 (46.0)	2.66%
	96	6.1 (1.6)	17.6 (41.7)	5.8 (1.5)	18.2 (43.2)	4.27%
	104	6.8 (1.8)	15.9 (37.7)	6.3 (1.7)	16.9 (40.1)	6.68%
	112	7.5 (2.0)	14.5 (34.4)	7.0 (1.8)	15.4 (36.6)	6.88%
	120	8.4 (2.2)	13.0 (30.9)	7.8 (2.1)	13.9 (33.0)	7.09%
3	72	5.3 (1.4)	20.1 (47.7)	5.2 (1.4)	20.1 (47.6)	1.35%
	80	5.4 (1.4)	19.5 (46.3)	5.4 (1.4)	19.7 (46.7)	0.87%
	88	5.8 (1.5)	18.5 (43.8)	5.6 (1.5)	18.8 (44.7)	3.26%
	96	6.3 (1.7)	17.0 (40.4)	6.0 (1.6)	17.7 (42.1)	4.98%
	104	7.0 (1.8)	15.5 (36.7)	6.5 (1.7)	16.5 (39.2)	7.03%
	112	7.7 (2.0)	14.1 (33.5)	7.1 (1.9)	15.1 (35.9)	7.18%
	120	8.6 (2.3)	12.8 (30.3)	8.0 (2.1)	13.6 (32.3)	7.10%

5.3.3 Calculations of Potential Annual Benefits

In order to quantify the potential annual benefits, the simulated fuel consumption rates (gallons/mile) were multiplied by the 2008 annual VMT by functional class [55]. Since a CC system cannot be engaged continuously, some assumptions were made; as follows:

- All rural interstate VMT are eligible for CC use because they were assumed to be congestion-free.
- The uncongested portion of the urban interstate VMT is eligible for CC use. Specifically, 45 percent of trips were considered to be uncongested trips based on the 2009 Mobility Report [56].
- 50 percent of rural arterial VMT are eligible because it was assumed that 50 percent of rural arterials perform the function of interstate highways and they are congestion-free.
- 22.5 percent of urban arterial VMT are eligible because it was assumed that 50 percent of urban arterials perform the function of interstate highways and 45 percent of them are congestion-free.

Given these assumptions, the CC-eligible VMT were calculated and summarized in Table 27 along with the total U.S. VMT.

Table 27: U.S. Total VMT (2008) and Cruise Control Eligible VMT

Classification	Urban VMT (million miles)		Rural VMT (million miles)	
	Total VMT	Cruise Control Eligible VMT	Total VMT	Cruise Control Eligible VMT
Interstate	476,091	214,241	243,290	243,290
Other arterials	1,062,226	239,001	374,273	187,137
Collector	175,389	-	241,158	-
Local	269,385	-	131,697	-
Total	1,983,091	453,242	990,418	430,427

The total CC-eligible VMT were then stratified by target speeds, as summarized in Table 28. The distribution of the target speeds was determined based on the distribution of the speed limits of the 50 states [57].

Table 28: Distribution of Cruise Control Eligible VMT by Target Speeds

Target Speed (km/h)	Urban Interstate		Urban Arterial		Rural Interstate		Rural Arterial	
	%	VMT (mile)	%	VMT (mile)	%	VMT (mile)	%	VMT (mile)
72	0%	0	2%	4780	0%	0	2%	3743
80	2%	4285	8%	19120	0%	0	8%	14971
88	24%	51418	50%	119500	0%	0	50%	93568
96	16%	34279	4%	9560	2%	4866	4%	7485
104	48%	102836	30%	71700	32%	77853	30%	56141
112	10%	21424	6%	14340	42%	102182	6%	11228
120	0%	0	0%	0	24%	58390	0%	0

Finally, the fuel consumption was calculated by multiplying the fuel consumption rates in gallons per mile by the total VMT for each of the target speeds. In addition, the fuel savings were estimated in gallons and in dollars. For the calculation, the gas price was assumed to be $3.00 per gallon. The potential annual benefits were demonstrated to be significant, as seen in Table 29. Specifically, the average potential fuel savings over the three scenarios were projected to be 1.04 billion gallons (or 33.5 million barrel) per year, which is equivalent to $3.12 billion saving per year. The results showed that the fuel savings were greater if the predictive ECC system is used in areas with hillier terrain (e.g. scenario-3) although the differences were within 0.5 percent. In addition, it would result in 9.20 million fewer metric tons of CO_2 released into the atmosphere, assuming that 1 L of fuel produces 2.33 kg of CO_2.

Table 29: Summary of Fuel Consumption and Fuel Saving

Classification		Total Fuel (million gallons)		Fuel Savings	
		Conventional Cruise	Predictive Cruise	million gallons	million dollars
Scenario-1	Urban Interstate	5,276	5,040	236 (4.5%)	707
	Urban Arterial	5,536	5,369	167 (3.0%)	502
	Rural Interstate	6,929	6,488	441 (6.4%)	1,322
	Rural Arterial	4,335	4,204	131 (3.0%)	393
	Total	**22,076**	**21,101**	**975 (4.4%)**	**2,924**
Scenario-2	Urban Interstate	5,397	5,151	246 (4.6%)	738
	Urban Arterial	5,677	5,494	183 (3.2%)	549
	Rural Interstate	7,046	6,615	431 (6.1%)	1,293
	Rural Arterial	4,445	4,302	143 (3.2%)	430
	Total	**22,566**	**21,562**	**1,004 (4.4%)**	**3,011**
Scenario-3	Urban Interstate	5,556	5,275	281 (5.1%)	844
	Urban Arterial	5,858	5,636	222 (3.8%)	666
	Rural Interstate	7,218	6,757	461 (6.4%)	1,382
	Rural Arterial	4,587	4,413	174 (3.8%)	522
	Total	**23,219**	**22,081**	**1,138 (4.9%)**	**3,415**

5.4 Conclusions

The study quantifies the potential benefits of the predictive ECC system relative to a conventional CC system considering various roadway grades. The study examined the impacts of using the predictive ECC system over an NYC to LA route and found that the system can save fuel consumption in the range of 4.7 to 6.7 percent without significantly increasing the travel time considering an ECC system with a +8 and -1.6 km/h speed range. The simulation results demonstrate that the introduction of a different speed range scheme can significantly improve the performance of the system, enhancing the vehicle fuel efficiency but with a potential increase in the total travel time. Similarly, the study also examined the effectiveness of the predictive ECC mode on a hilly rural interstate highway section, which contains the maximum grade of 4 percent and the maximum downhill grade of 5 percent. The study found when test vehicles utilized the predictive ECC system with a speed range of +8 and -1.6 km/h, the fuel efficiency was increased by 9.0 percent on average with less than a 1-percent speed changes compared to the conventional CC trip.

The study also found that heavy vehicles (e.g. Ford F150) can generally achieve more fuel savings when compared to light vehicles (e.g. Toyota Corolla) and the benefits of the predictive ECC system are maximized when vehicles travel on hilly terrains. In addition, the predictive ECC system saves more fuel when the test vehicles are operated at higher target speeds rather than lower target speeds. However, the test vehicles showed the best fuel efficiencies at the target speed of 72 km/h.

The simulation study found that the U.S. could save approximately 1.04 billion gallons (or 33.5 million barrel) per year, when the predictive ECC system is applied to all vehicles in the United States. The average potential cost savings were projected to be $3.12 billion per year when assuming that the price of gasoline is $3.0 per gallon. In addition, the ECC system can result in 9.2 million fewer metric tons of CO_2 released into the atmosphere, assuming that 1 liter of fuel produces 2.33 kg of CO_2.

6. CONCLUSIONS AND RECOMMENDATIONS FOR FURTHER RESEARCH

6.1 Summary of the Research

The research presented in this report builds a framework for developing a predictive ECC system that can control vehicle speed within a pre-set speed range to minimize vehicle fuel consumption and CO_2 emission levels using roadway topographic information. The study includes five basic tasks: (a) develop a vehicle powertrain model that can be easily implemented within eco-driving tools; (b) develop a simple fuel consumption model that uses instantaneous vehicle power; (c) evaluate manual driving and conventional CC driving using field-collected data; (d) develop a predictive ECC system that uses roadway grade information with the developed vehicle powertrain and fuel consumption models; and (e) evaluate the potential benefits of using the predictive ECC system. Key input variables to the predictive ECC system include roadway grade information obtained from a high resolution digital map, a target speed, and a maximum and minimum speed range. The results of this study support the following conclusions:

a. The research developed a simple vehicle powertrain model that can be integrated with car-following models within microscopic traffic simulation software. This simple model can be calibrated using engine and powertrain parameters that are publicly available without the need for field data collection. The model uses the driver throttle-level input to compute the engine speed; model the transmission system (manual and automatic); and compute the vehicle's acceleration, speed, and position. The model was demonstrated to produce vehicle acceleration, speed, position, and fuel consumption estimates that are consistent with field observations.

b. The study develops two simple fuel consumption models that do not result in a bang-bang control system and that can be calibrated easily using publicly available data. Specifically, the models can be calibrated using the EPA city and highway fuel economy ratings that are publicly available. The new fuel consumption model is entitled the Virginia Tech Comprehensive Power-based Fuel Consumption Model (VT-CPFM). Instantaneous vehicle power is used as a single input variable to estimate a vehicle fuel consumption level. The models are demonstrated to estimate vehicle fuel consumption rates consistent with in-field measurements (coefficient of determination above 0.90). In addition, a procedure for estimating CO_2 emissions is developed, producing emission estimates that are highly correlated with field measurements (greater than 0.98).

c. The study validated the VT-CPFMs by comparing field-measured fuel consumption rates with model estimates. The results demonstrated that the VT-CPFM model calibrated using the city and highway fuel economy ratings provide reliable fuel consumption estimates. More importantly, both estimates and measurements produce identical responses to engine load levels. The proposed model can be integrated within a traffic simulation framework to quantify the energy and environmental impacts of traffic operational projects.

d. The study compared conventional CC with manual driving with regard to fuel economy using field tests. The study found that the CC driving improves fuel efficiency as compared to manual driving although there were some variations in the differences depending on the driver, the vehicle, and the direction of travel. Based on the test results, CC driving resulted in a fuel economy enhancement ranging from 0.2% to 10.5% when compared to manual driving. The average fuel economy enhancement across all the field tests was 3.3 percent; however, this was not statistically significant.

e. This study developed a predictive ECC system that controls vehicle speed within a pre-set speed range to minimize the vehicle's fuel consumption. The predictive ECC system consists of three components: a fuel consumption module, a powertrain module, and an optimization algorithm. The performance of the system is tested by simulating a vehicle trip on a section of Interstate 81 in the state of Virginia. The results demonstrate fuel savings of up to 15 percent with execution times within real time. The simulation made assumptions for an easier interpretation of the system performance, including: no errors in the vehicle control, topographical information feeding, and no interference by other vehicles.

f. The study also examined the impacts of using the predictive ECC system over a New York City to Los Angeles route and found that the system can save fuel consumption in the range of 4.7 to 6.7 percent without increasing the total travel time (considering a speed range of +8 and -1.6 km/h). The simulation results demonstrate that the introduction of a different speed range scheme during the predictive ECC trips can significantly improve the performance of the system, improving vehicle fuel efficiency without increasing the total travel time.

g. The study also found that heavy vehicles (e.g. Ford F150) can generally achieve more fuel savings when compared to light vehicles (e.g. Toyota Corolla) with the predictive ECC system and the benefits of the predictive ECC system are maximized when vehicles travel on hilly terrains. In addition, the predictive ECC system saves more fuel when the test vehicles are operated at higher target speeds rather than lower target speeds.

h. The simulation study found if a predictive ECC system is applied to all vehicles in the United States, the average potential fuel savings were projected to be 1.04 billion gallons per year, which is equivalent to $3.12 billion per year when assuming that the price of gasoline is $3.00 per gallon. In addition, the ECC system can result in 9.2 million fewer metric tons of CO_2 released into the atmosphere, assuming that 1 liter of fuel produces 2.33 kg of CO_2.

6.2 Further Research

The following areas of research should be pursued to expand the applicability of the eco-driving modeling framework developed in the context of predictive ECC system:

a. The developed predictive ECC system assumes that there is no interaction with other vehicles. Further research should consider the interactions with other vehicles to quantify the potential benefits of the system.

b. The study should be expanded to investigate the potential nationwide benefits of using the proposed system that can interact with other vehicles by facility type, speed limit, congestion levels, and location type (urban/rural area). The categorized fuel savings data will be generalized in order to estimate the potential nationwide benefits. The reduced GHG emissions will be converted to cost savings and will be combined with fuel cost savings in order to estimate the total nationwide benefits of the eco-driving system.

c. Future study should design and develop the optimum user interface to convey the information provided from the predictive ECC system to the driver. The research should (1) identify system functionality and the user interface, (2) utilize human factors and driving safety design principles to identify candidate feedback interfaces, (3) develop prototype interfaces for on-road testing and design experiments, and (4) conduct on-road experiments to evaluate the performance of drivers with the algorithm and prototype interfaces in order to develop the user interface.

d. After completing the development of the user interface, the hardware should be developed and implemented into test vehicles. The field test will be performed to identify driving behavior and to study the adaptability of the predictive ECC system.

REFERENCES

1. Rakha, H., M. Snare, and F. Dion, *Vehicle dynamics model for estimating maximum light-duty vehicle acceleration levels.* Transportation Research Record, 2004. n 1883: p. 40-49.
2. Rakha, H. and I. Lucic, *Variable power vehicle dynamics model for estimating maximum truck acceleration levels.* Journal of Transportation Engineering, 2002. 128(5): p. 412-419.
3. Ni, D. and D. Henclewood, *Simple Engine Models for VII-Enabled In-Vehicle Applications.* IEEE Transactions on Vehicular Technology, 2008. 57(5): p. 2695-2702.
4. Cicero-Fernandez, P., J.R. Long, and A.M. Winer, *Effects of grades and other loads on on-road emissions of hydrocarbons and carbon monoxide.* Journal of the Air & Waste Management Association, 1997. 47(8): p. 898-904.
5. Park, S. and H. Rakha, *Energy and Environmental Impacts of Roadway Grades.* Transportation Research Record, 2006(1987): p. 13.
6. Boriboonsomsin, K. and M. Barth. *Fuel and CO2 Impacts from Advanced Navigation Systems that Account for Road Grade. Presented at 88th Annual Meeting of the Transportation Research Board.* 2009. Washington, D.C.
7. Ahn, K. and H. Rakha, *The effects of route choice decisions on vehicle energy consumption and emissions.* Transportation Research. Part D, Transport and environment, 2008. 13(3): p. 17.
8. Powell, B.K., *A dynamic model for automotive engine control analysis.* Proc. 18th IEEE Conf. Decision Control, 1979: p. 120.
9. Powell, J.D., *A review of IC engine models for control system design.* Proc. Int. Federation Automat. Control, 1987.
10. Dobner, D.J., *A mathematical engine model for development of dynamic engine control.* Society of Automotive Engineers, 1980. no 800054.
11. Moskwa, J.J. and J.K. Hedrick. *Automotive engine modeling for real time control application.* in *Proceedings of the 1987 American Control Conference, pp. 341-346* 1987. Minneapolis.
12. Yoon, P. and M. Sunwoo, *A nonlinear dynamic modelling of SI engines for controller design.* International Journal of Vehicle Design, 2001. 26: p. 277-297.
13. Cho, D. and J.K. Hedrick, *Automotive powertrain modeling for control.* Trans. ASME, J. Dyn. Syst. Meas. Control, 1989. 111: p. 568-576.
14. Guzzella, L. and A. Sciarretta, *Vehicle Propulsion Systems - Introduction to Modeling and Optimization.* 2nd ed. 2007, New York: Springer.
15. Kiencke, U. and L. Nielsen, *Automotive control systems : for engine, driveline, and vehicle.* 2nd. ed. 2005, Berlin u.a.: Springer. XVIII, 512 S.
16. Rakha, H., P. Pasumarthy, and S. Adjerid. *The INTEGRATION framework for modeling longitudinal vehicle motion.* in *TRANSTEC.* 2004. Athens, Greece.
17. Rakha, H., P. Pasumarthy, and S. Adjerid. *Modeling longitudinal vehicle motion: issues and proposed solutions.* in *Transport Science and Technology Congress.* 2004. Athens, Greece.
18. Wong, J.Y., *Theory of Ground Vehicles, 3rd Edition.* 2001: Wiley.
19. Genta, G., *Motor Vehicle Dynamics: Modeling and Simulation*, in *World Scientific.* 2003.
20. Rakha, H., I. Lucic, S.H. Demarchi, J.R. Setti, and M. Van Aerde, *Vehicle dynamics model for predicting maximum truck acceleration levels.* Journal of Transportation Engineering, 2001. 127(5): p. 418-425.

21.   McKinsey & Company, *Roads toward a low-carbon future: Reducing CO2 emissions from passenger vehicles in the global road transportation system.* 2009.

22.   Saerens, B., M. Diehl, and E. Van den Bulck, *Automotive Model Predictive Control: Models, Methods and Applications,* in *Lecture Notes in Control and Information Sciences.* 2010, Springer: Berlin / Heidelberg. p. 119-138.

23.   Post, K., J.H. Kent, J. Tomlin, and N. Carruthers, *Fuel consumption and emission modeling by power demand and a comparison with other model.* Transportation Research, 1984. 18A: p. 191-213.

24.   Akcelik, R., *Efficiency and drag in the power-based model of fuel consumption.* Transportation Research Part B-Methodological, 1989. 23B(5): p. 376-385.

25.   Fisk, C.S., *Australian Road Research Board instantaneous model of fuel consumption.* Transportation Research Part B-Methodological, 1989. 23B(5): p. 373-376.

26.   Barth, M., F. An, J. Norbeck, and M. Ross, *Modal emissions modeling: A physical approach.* Transportation Research Record, 1996(1520): p. 81-88.

27.   Barth, M., F. An, T. Younglove, G. Scora, C. Levine, M. Ross, and T. Wenzel, *Comprehensive modal emission model (CMEM), version 2.0 user's guide.* 2000, Riverside, CA.

28.   Froberg, A., E. Hellstrom, and L. Nielsen, *Explicit Fuel Optimal Speed Profiles for Heavy Trucks on a Set of Topographic Road Profiles.* SAE International, 2006. 2006-01-1071.

29.   Hellinga, B. and L. Fu, *Assessing Expected Accuracy of Probe Vehicle Travel Time Reports.* Journal of Transportation Engineering, 1999. 125(6): p. 7.

30.   Hellinga, B., M.A. Khan, and L. Fu. *Analytical Emission Models for Signalised Arterials* in *The Canadian Society of Civil Engineers 3rd Transportation Specialty Conference.* 2000. London, Ontario, CA.

31.   Hellinga, B.R., *Improving Freeway Speed Estimates from Single-Loop Detectors.* Journal of Transportation Engineering, 2002. 128(1): p. 10.

32.   Ahn, K., H. Rakha, A. Trani, and M. Van Aerde, *Estimating vehicle fuel consumption and emissions based on instantaneous speed and acceleration levels.* Journal of Transportation Engineering-ASCE, 2002. 128(2): p. 182-190.

33.   Rakha, H., K. Ahn, and A. Trani, *Development of VT-Micro model for estimating hot stabilized light duty vehicle and truck emissions.* Transportation Research, Part D: Transport & Environment, 2004. 9(1): p. 49-74.

34.   Wong, J.Y., *Theory of Ground Vehicles.* Third ed. 2001: John Wiley & Sons, Inc.

35.   Ross, M., *Fuel efficiency and the physics of automobiles.* Contemporary Physics, 1997. 38(6): p. 381-394.

36.   Edgar, J., *Brake Specific Fuel Consumption, issue 475,* in *Autospeed.* 2008: http://autospeed.com/cms/A_110216/article.html.

37.   West, B., R. McGill, J. Hodgson, S. Sluder, and D. Smith, *Development of Data-Based Light-Duty Modal Emissions and Fuel Consumption Models.* Society of Automotive Engineers, 1997. 972910.

38.   Rakha, H., K. Ahn, K. Moran, B. Saerens, and E.V.d. Bulck, *Virginia Tech Comprehensive Power-Based Fuel Consumption Model: Model development and testing* Transportation Research. Part D, Transport and Environment, 2011. 16(7): p. 492-503

39.   Rakha, H.A., K. Ahn, K. Moran, B. Saerens, and E.V.d. Bulck, *Virginia Tech Comprehensive Power-Based Fuel Consumption Model: Model development and testing.*

Transportation Research Part D: Transportation and Environment, 2011. Volume 16(Issue 7): p. 492-503.

40. Drew Technologies Inc., *DashDAQ Series II - Instruction Manual*. 2010.

41. Ahn, K., H. Rakha, A. Trani, and M. Van Aerde, *Estimating vehicle fuel consumption and emissions based on instantaneous speed and acceleration levels.* Journal of Transportation Engineering, 2002. 128(2): p. 182-190.

42. Rakha, H., M. Van Aerde, K. Ahn, and A.A. Trani, *Requirements for evaluating traffic signal control impacts on energy and emissions based on instantaneous speed and acceleration measurements.* Transportation Research Record. n 1738 2000, 2000: p. 56-67 00-1133.

43. *Driving More Efficiently.* [cited 2011 August]; Available from: fueleconomy.gov/feg/driveHabits.shtml.

44. Park, S., H. Rakha, K. Ahn, and K. Moran, *Predictive Eco-cruise Control System: Model Logic and Preliminary Testing.* Presented at 91st Annual Meeting of the Transportation Research Board, Washington, D.C., 2012.

45. Ellis, D. *4 gas-saving myths.* 2007; Available from: http://money.cnn.com/2007/05/09/pf/gas_myths/index.htm.

46. Natural Resources Canada. *Auto$mart Thinking - Driving and Maintaining Your Vehicle.* Available from: http://oee.nrcan.gc.ca/transportation/personal/driving/2578.

47. Fekpe, E. and D. Gopalakrishna, *Traffic Data Quality Workshop Proceedings and Action Plan.* 2003, Prepared for Federal Highway Administration: Washington, D.C.

48. Davis, S.C. and S.W. Diegel, *Transportation Energy Data Book: Edition 26.* 2007, Oak Ridge National Laboratory.

49. Hellstrom, E., *Explicit use of road topography for model predictive cruise control in heavy trucks*, in *Dept. of Electrical Engineering.* 2005, Linkopings Universitet.

50. Rakha, H., K. Ahn, K. Moran, B. Saerens, and E.V.d. Bulck, *Simple Comprehensive Fuel Consumption and CO_2 Emissions Model based on Instantaneous Vehicle Power.* Presented at 90th Annual Meeting of the Transportation Research Board, Washington D.C., 2011.

51. Hellstrom, E., *Explicit use of road topography for model predictive cruise control in heavy trucks*, in *Electrical Engineering.* 2005, Linkopings Universitet: Linkoping. p. 43.

52. Dijkstra, E.W., *A Note on Two Problems in Connexion with Graphs.* Numerische Mathematik, 1959. 1: p. 269-271.

53. Rakha, H., K. Ahn, K. Moran, B. Saerens, and E.V.d. Bulck, *Simple Comprehensive Fuel Consumption and CO2 Emissions Model based on Instantaneous Vehicle Power.* Transportation Research Board 90th Annual Meeting, Washington, D.C., 2011.

54. Ahn, K., H. Rakha, and K. Moran, *Eco-Cruise Control: Feasibility and Initial Testing.* Presented at 90th Annual Meeting of the Transportation Research Board, Washington, D.C., 2011.

55. U.S. Department of Transportation, *National Transportation Statistics 2010.* 2010.

56. Schrank, D. and T. Lomax, *2009 Urban Mobility Report, Texas Transportation Institute.* 2009.

57. Federal Highway Administration, *Advanced Parking Management Systems: A Cross-Cutting Study.* 2007: Washington, D.C.

www.ingramcontent.com/pod-product-compliance
Lightning Source LLC
Chambersburg PA
CBHW081841280526
45789CB00007B/2530